Contemplating

Christ and Creation

30 Days

Charlotte Bowden

God bless you.
with love
Charlotte B.

ISBN: 9798323288656

Dedication

For those who want to know Father, Son and Holy Spirit and fall deeper in love with God.
For those who desire to explore silence and contemplation.

Contents

Acknowledgements

Firstly, I acknowledge the loving grace of our Lord Jesus Christ, who strengthens us with power through his Spirit in our inner being, so that Christ dwells in our hearts through faith. He is the One who roots and establishes us in love, and he desires to fill us with the fullness of his immeasurable love.

Thank you to St. Ignatius of Loyola and his writing of the *Spiritual Exercises*, and to all who were involved in taking me through the 30 days at St Beuno's in Wales. Special thanks to Ken for being such a great friend.

I am grateful to Maureen Menard, Director of Christian Formation and Discipleship, University of the Nations, who led the M.A programme, which initiated my writing this book. Many thanks to Dr. John Peachey, my supervisor for this final project, and all the staff, students, and teachers, for their love and encouragement throughout the degree. Thank you to the Youth With A Mission (YWAM) campus I work with, for their love and support as they implemented these contemplations into their agenda and encouraged me with their feedback.

Special thanks to Sally Raynham, who has been invaluable with her advice and skill in copy editing this book.

Contemplating Christ and Creation

Introduction

Prayer, Silence, and Solitude

Prayer was the foundation of Jesus' ministry. He often went to lonely places to pray[1] and be with his Father. He encouraged his disciples to do likewise, since he said to them, "Come away by yourselves to a desolate place and rest a while".[2] For us to abide in Christ, we too need to escape the hurry and noise of the world, and withdraw to a place of silence and solitude, to recharge and abide in Jesus without the distractions.

Being in silence is not without its challenges. Some find it hard to turn off their phones, are easily distracted, or feel they need to have something to do. It can be quite alien to sit and meditate on scripture and be with Christ in silence or reflect on him and listen to him speaking in the quiet. But when all the distractions are taken away, we can notice how we feel; how tired we might be; how anxious we are; how out of tune we feel with Christ. As we give up our doing, and seek Christ as he seeks us, we are nourished and transformed.

Even Jesus, who walked in close communion with his Father, needed alone-time with him away from all the activity of the world. For us, it can be difficult to lay aside daily, quality, alone time with God, as we are caught up in the busyness of the task of serving God and others, but if we do not, we will find ourselves working for God in our own strength and wearing ourselves out. As we spend time with Jesus, we can listen to what is going on within us and notice our selfish desires and habits. We can offer ourselves to Christ for transformation, rather than be transformed by our sinful nature or by others. Jesus does not transform us when we are on the run, but when we seek him and desire to be with him and receive from him. The more we are in the habit of constantly being in Christ in silence, the more we will be able to live by the Holy Spirit, despite the busyness of the world.

Spending time in silence and outside in God's creation is a way of leaving the hurry of everyday life, and contemplating the beauty of God's created world, enabling us to listen to him amidst the sunshine,

9

wind, and birds. I am aware of how God speaks to us in nature, having experienced this first-hand, and I am not alone in this. Elijah (1 Kings 19:9-18), King David (Psalm 19) and Jesus (John 15:1-11, Mark 4:1-20, 26-34) are a few of the people mentioned in the Bible who sensed God's presence in creation. Reading from the church fathers, ancient and modern contemplatives, and from my own experience, I noticed that Christian formation takes place in silence, in creation, and in listening and talking with God, along with talking about God with others in community. Henri Nouwen, the Dutch priest, writer, and theologian wrote, "Without solitude it is virtually impossible to live a spiritual life."[3]

Christian Formation and Discipleship

Christian formation is a slow, life-long learning process. It involves us being present to God as we open ourselves to his transforming power. In our partnership with God, we do not need to try to be a better person. As we acknowledge our faults in repentance to him, and allow him to gently sanctify us, he is the one who changes us for the better. As we notice Holy Spirit transforming our mind and heart, our love for him deepens. For Christian formation to occur and to know Christ more deeply, we need to resist those activities and desires we love, but which are not transformational, and spend time with the Lord. We need to evaluate what we want to do, or what the world, culture and others desire us to do, and listen to what the Holy Spirit desires for us. This is a choice. This process of living by the Holy Spirit takes time, patience, and discernment as each of us understands the focus is not on us, but on what Holy Spirit is doing within us. An intimacy with Christ occurs through those times of being with him in quietness and contemplation. As with any relationship, I believe it is essential for anyone desiring to deepen their relationship with Christ, to spend quality time with the One they love.

The aim of Christian formation is to become Christ-like in our nature, beliefs, and actions. The great disciple and apostle, Paul, plays a key role in explaining how we can become like Christ. He wrote,

"It is no longer I who live, but Christ who lives in me.
And the life I now live in the flesh I live by faith in the
Son of God, who loved me and gave himself for me."[4]

In his letters, he teaches and encourages Christian communities to set their minds on the Holy Spirit, who gives life and transforms man's sinful nature to a Christ-like nature. Apart from God, people are self-centred, desiring to live contrary to God's way, which brings spiritual death and deformity.[5]

We are formed by a true understanding of the Trinitarian God: Father, Son, and Holy Spirit and the God-inspired words of the Bible. God's word was not given to us as interesting historical information, but it is "living and active ... discerning the thoughts and intentions of the heart".[6] As we reflect on God's word, we learn who God is and how to live, and the Holy Spirit transforms us in our understanding, so we desire to live according to God's ways.

Christian formation requires us to keep company with Father, Son, and Holy Spirit and this takes time and practice. We can accompany Jesus through reading and being with him through his word. But there are many people who read the Bible and do not know Jesus. The two men on the road to Emmaus were taught the scriptures by Jesus on their journey and invited him to their home, but they did not recognise Jesus until he "took the bread and blessed and broke it and gave it to them. And then their eyes were opened, and they recognized him."[7] Christian formation will not take place within the context of reading the word unless the Holy Spirit opens our eyes to the text, reveals the truth, and forms us as we travel through the words with him.

As we engage with Holy Spirit and understand God's role within the biblical story, we become more aware of God's presence within us and within our ministry. Christ, by the Holy Spirit, forms us through this engagement and understanding, and as we encourage and teach others to see God within the Bible, so we assist in the Christian formation of others. The Bible helps us know why we live, how to live and what we are living for as we struggle with sin, death, and the principalities of darkness. The Spirit brings light and truth to situations and shows the lies that do not come from a loving God but come from the devil or from human selfishness. Through the life of Christ in the biblical story, we see how he has always been there from the beginning, always desiring to dwell with us and show us what it is to be fully human and fully alive. Through repeated themes, he shows us how he is the fulfilment of the Covenant of God, how he continues to save us from slavery, how he is the true Temple of God and why he needed to come. If we do not keep God and scripture at the forefront of our lives, we can end up doing what we feel or desire and find we are just living for ourselves, rather than in Christ and his purpose for us.

The implication of understanding God as three persons: Father, Son, and Holy Spirit and calling them by name, rather than *simply* God, can help us understand the personal nature of each and their distinct role. You will notice I usually write Holy Spirit, rather than the Holy Spirit, to emphasise his third personhood in the Trinity. Understanding the communion of love between the Trinity, which existed before creation, is key to understanding how loved and included we are with Father, Son, and Holy Spirit. It is out of that abounding love that we are invited into the purposes of the Father, through Jesus Christ, by Holy Spirit. If a disciple only understands that sin has come into the world and there is a need to be saved from sin they can miss out on the immense love of the Father, Son, and Spirit for them. In their desire to know God, they can end up trying to work for God, because they have been told that they have a role to play, or in trying to please God. All the self-effort can lead to exhaustion and/or falling away from an apparently impersonal being they have no relationship with. Or they may create their own God in their mind and heart and follow their own desires that they attribute to God.

We are formed through spiritual practices or disciplines, which draw us into Christ's presence. These disciplines include fasting, meditation, prayer, contemplating Christ and the scripture, silence and solitude, study, liturgy, sabbath rest and worship. As we spend time with Christ through these disciplines we create a daily routine, and this draws us away from the desires of the world and our sinful nature and into the presence of God. They contribute to transforming our mind so we can discern God's will and his purpose for us in the world.[8] If we are not being transformed by Christ, we will be transformed by our culture and the world around us which can draw us away from God. Christian practices enable us to engage with Father, Son, and Spirit, and to deepen our understanding and wisdom in who we are in Christ.

The most valuable company we keep is with Father, Son, and Holy Spirit, but also there are all those people who lived before us who were formed by God and those who travel with us. We journey with the writers of the Bible, who talked with God and heard directly from him and those who walked with Jesus under his discipleship. We walk with those early Christian fathers and mothers, friends of friends of those who knew Jesus and we can listen to them and learn through their writings, along with contemporary writers. As we accompany all these creative companions of expression from past and present, we also partner with those near to us with whom we talk face-to-face and who shape us by their presence and closeness - as we shape them.

The Motivation for this Book

Contemplating Christ and Creation was originally written as a research project for a master's degree in Christian Formation and Discipleship with the University of the Nations. The project was created to take place over 30 days. It incorporated 30 written contemplations, based on the biblical story of Christ and creation, combined with meditation on scripture, questions for reflection, poems, and reflection on each day with the *Examen* prayer. The motivation for this project came from my love and belief in the value of being with Christ in silence and meditation, reflection on scripture and God's beauty in creation. I have regularly embraced silent retreats in various locations, where I have spent extended times in silence and solitude, along with talking to a guide once a day about what God is doing within me. I have found these times, away from the busyness of life, to be transforming as my mind focuses on Jesus alone, and I experience his presence.

In the summer of 2017, I went to St Beuno's Jesuit Spirituality Centre in Wales, where I spent 30 days in silent contemplation and prayer, doing the *Spiritual Exercises of Saint Ignatius of Loyola*. For centuries Jesuit missionaries have been making this 30-day retreat at least once in their lifetime, and it is noted to be of great benefit to them in deepening their life with Christ and discerning their purpose and mission. Ignatian spirituality recognises that we are in a relationship with God, created in God's image[9] and as created living beings we have a connection with all of God's living creation. We are not merely stewards of creation, but we "share in God's authority, a real part in establishing, maintaining, healing, and restoring creation."[10] We can only do this if we learn to love God, love ourselves and others and all God's creation, and see our relationship within this.

The *Spiritual Exercises* incorporate 30 days of silence and reflection on Jesus and the biblical story. Ignatius' writing covers God's love for creation and our response, the issue of evil and sin and our need for healing and forgiveness, discipleship, the passion of Christ, the resurrection, our response to God's love, and thankfulness for his gifts. Using the Bible and the 30-day spiritual exercises retreat, which included many helpful handouts by Robert R. Marsh S.J.,* as the backbone to these 30 days of contemplation, I incorporated what most impacted me from every module of the Christian formation and discipleship master's degree.

The aim of the project was for participants to reflect with Christ on a contemplation, scripture, poem and the *Examen*, and notice Christ's presence within them. The goal of this slow process of silence and reflection, along with listening and feedback within a small group, was that each participant might see their life deepen in love with Christ, and with others, and reveal the discipline of silence and contemplation on a YWAM campus as an important asset to Christian formation. The project revealed how a community of Christian missionaries from different countries, but living in the UK, were impacted, individually and corporately, to be more aware of Christ's presence through the silent reflection days.

Although it was designed for each person to go through the reflections individually, there was also the opportunity for those reflecting to talk with others about what Christ was doing within them. This was an opportunity for all involved to notice resistance or acceptance of each practice as they invited the Holy Spirit to speak to them through this process of contemplation. As they reflected on the contemplations and then talked together, my hope was they would become more aware of Christ's presence in their lives and his love for them and all of creation. My desire was they would recognise an intimacy with Christ through those times of quietness and contemplation, which would encourage them to continue this practice of silence and contemplation.

---

* Society of Jesus, which was founded by Ignatius of Loyola in 1540

Preparation for the Days Ahead

You might like to go through this book with a group of trusted friends, or family, and meet occasionally to talk about your experience. This can be an opportunity to share where you notice resistance or acceptance of any of the practices, and encourage one another, as you share your life together.

If you have time, you may like to go through one day at a time, taking thirty days to cover the book. Alternatively, you can go through the material more slowly, maybe over a week for each day, especially if you have other commitments. You may like to read and reflect on the contemplation on the first day. The second day, with the contemplation in mind, you can consider the reflection and questions. You could do the practical on the same day or another day. You might want to reflect on the poem in the evening. The scripture could be reflected on another day.

The main emphasis is to go slowly through the book in a way that serves you. It is not meant to be rushed through and devoured like a great novel, but slowly absorbed so it nourishes and transforms you, and makes you think and reflect on Christ, your life, and creation. I suggest that whatever method you use for going through the book, that you do the *Examen* prayer at some point during the day or evening. The *Examen* prayer helps you to discern what God is doing through your life, understand your identity in Christ, and how he has gifted you.

You will notice that I have not written out most of the poems, due to copyright, but I have written the name of the poem and author, as they can be easily found on the internet. I encourage you to look them up and ponder on them, as they are rich in word and thought. Any scripture quoted is taken from the English Standard Version (ESV) of the Holy Bible, unless otherwise specified.

Traditional Practices

Spending time with God is a discipline that takes time away from the world and the lives we live with others. I believe, to be fruitful in our ministry, it is this sacrifice of being with God in silence, which enables us to serve him.

You will notice that the prayer times include terms, such as *Lectio Divina*, *Imaginative Prayer* and *Examen*. You may be familiar with these ways of prayer, but if you are not, the following may help you to understand these ancient practices still in use today.

Lectio Divina[†]

Lectio Divina is Latin for "Divine Reading", and Christians have been using this method of praying with scripture for centuries. It is a method of slowly going through a passage of scripture, and chewing over it, reflecting, and enjoying the goodness. It is like enjoying an excellent meal, savouring the delicious flavours and then swallowing and letting the taste linger, before moving on to the next bite. These are the stages of *Lectio Divina*, which flow from one to the other:

1. Choose the scripture passage you plan to pray.
2. Place yourself in a comfortable position in a quiet place where you can be attentive to God.
3. Recognise you are sitting in God's loving presence, and he looks at you with love.
4. Reflect on how you are feeling and bring that to God in prayer and pray for God's grace as you reflect on the scripture passage.
5. Slowly read the scripture and stop if a word or phrase speaks to you. Stay with that word or phrase for as long as it speaks to you. You might want to talk to God about the word or phrase or be silent before him.
6. When you have finished listening to God within the word or passage, then move on with the reading.
7. If, at any time, your thoughts wander off and you get distracted, that is fine. That might indicate it is time to move on with the reading. It also might be an indication to ask for God's grace to bring you back to the passage.
8. When your prayer time has finished, due to time or you have finished the passage, you might like to say a prayer to God to thank him for being with you and speaking to you.
9. It is good to journal or draw what God has spoken to you as a reminder of his speaking and so you can go back to it.
10. Remember to take your time with this kind of "Divine Reading", expectant that God will speak to you through the

---

† Based on a handout courtesy of St. Beuno's, Ignatian Spirituality Centre.

passage.

11. *Lectio Divina* is not so much about studying the scriptures and using the mind, but more about engaging the feelings and listening to God, as you prayerfully read and let the scriptures speak to you.

Imaginative Prayer[‡]

Imaginative Prayer, Gospel Contemplation or *Ignatian Contemplation* are different names for the same method of meditation that is best suited with the stories in the gospels. This type of prayer engages the imagination into the story of Jesus' life, so we enter the story with our mind and emotions and imagine ourselves there. It can reveal what is hidden in our subconscious mind, but which Christ might raise to the surface, as we reflect. We might feel angry or sad or joyful as we engage in the story, which might tell us something about what is going on deep within us.

The writer and Jesuit Priest, Gerard W. Hughes, explains this kind of prayer in *God of Surprises*. He describes a pilgrim he met with who meditated on John chapter 2, the wedding at Cana. The pilgrim reflected on the scene and imagined himself being at the wedding where there was merriment and dancing. When Hughes asked him to describe what Jesus was like, he portrayed a figure who was disapproving of what was going on. The pilgrim discovered an image of God in his subconscious mind which he was unaware of, but which was influencing his life. Once he discerned this wrong image, he was able to understand who God really was and let that mould his mind and heart.

Contemplating a passage of scripture, using *Imaginative Prayer*, means setting the imagination free to enter the passage and be there in the scene, interacting with the characters, or being one of them. It is not so much about discerning the truth of the text, but discovering what is happening within you, and how Jesus is speaking to you. So how do we engage with this kind of prayer? Here are some points to help you engage with *Imaginative Prayer*.

1. Choose the gospel passage you plan to pray.
2. Place yourself in a comfortable position in a quiet place where

---

‡ Based on a handout, courtesy of St. Beuno's, Ignatian Spirituality Centre.

you can be attentive to God.

3. Recognise you are sitting in God's loving presence, and he looks at you with love. You might like to pray this Ignatian preparatory prayer:

   Direct, O Lord, guide, and influence all that is happening in my mind and heart during this time of prayer, all my moods and feelings, my memories, and imaginings; may all be directed and influenced to your greater service and to my growth in the Spirit. Amen.

4. Reflect on how you are feeling and bring that to God in prayer and pray for God's grace as you reflect on the scripture passage. You might want to pray for his grace or gift to know Jesus more intimately or to have compassion or feel you are sharing in his suffering. On the days which include this kind of prayer, I indicate what you can ask. If your mind drifts during the meditation, it can help to ask Jesus again for this specific grace of gift, trusting that he will draw you back into his presence.

5. Read the gospel passage, aloud, if possible, two to five times until you have the story in your imagination. After each reading you might like to pause for a minute and imagine the scene, so you start to remember it as it sinks into your imagination. After each reading you will remember more details as they settle into your imagination. As you read and imagine, let your mind be engrossed in the story so that distractions disappear.

6. Put the Bible aside and attentively imagine what is going on in the story and let it play out. You might listen to the wind, the birds, or people shouting, smell the Sea of Galilee, the fish, or a charcoal fire. You might drift into the scene and touch Jesus. Let the story unfold as you reflect on what is happening. You might find yourself in the scene as yourself or you might imagine yourself as one of the characters. You might want to ask Jesus a question and listen to his response or you might interact with one of the other characters. The aim is to remain alert to what is happening, letting it unfold, in your imagination. Let it happen without making any judgement or attempting to draw a theological conclusion. The time you spend on this is up to you. You may like to spend ten minutes

initially and in time you may like to sit with a passage for an hour.

7. As you come to the end of this prayer time, you might like to talk to Jesus and thank him for spending time with you.

8. When you have finished this prayer time, you may like to journal what has been going on and how Jesus has spoken to you, so you do not forget. It is not uncommon for us to have insight from God that enters our minds as we reflect on scripture. I encourage you not to start writing before you end your time of prayer, as it can disturb what God is doing within you. If God is speaking, what he is saying will stay with you, and even deepen as you contemplate.

Examen

A daily *Examen*, which is a discipline I incorporated into the contemplations, helps us discern God's guidance in our lives. This form of prayer helps us notice when we are living with God, and when we are living away from God following the ways of the world or our own desires. It helps us look at our identity, where we put our security, and reflect on all aspects of our life. As we offer what we notice to God, we allow him to transform us and move us forward in our Christian spirituality.

The *Examen* is a centuries-old form of prayer which invites God to speak to us through our deepest feelings. St. Ignatius, who wrote the *Spiritual Exercises*, insisted that all those who joined the Society of Jesus, which he founded, engaged in this form of listening to God. He felt this was vital to their spiritual life as a way of discerning how they were drawn into God's presence and how they were drawn away from God's presence. It is a very simple process of taking time each day to ask yourself two questions, which can be asked in different ways. The questions for reflection are to ask yourself for what you are most grateful and for what you are least grateful, and to bring those times before God in prayer. Through identifying these moments, people have found direction for their day and life, and they continue to do so. We can ask the same question by asking what gives life to us and what drains life from us. This might be a task we do, or a person we talk with, or a place we visit. What gives life to one person, such as being with a crowd of people talking, might drain life from another, who receives life from quiet and spending time alone.

It can be good to do this kind of prayer at the end of the day as you reflect on the day, or first thing in the morning as you reflect on the previous day. You might light a candle as you reflect on Jesus, who is "the light of the world",[11] and who gives you divine revelation. He constantly talks to you and reveals himself to you throughout your day. It is for us to notice this relationship.

Simply, with Jesus, reflect on your day and what brought you joy and love and what drained you of joy and love. It is something you can do by yourself, or you can do it with others. However you do this, you bring your findings to God in prayer, without judgement, but just noticing how he is at work within you.

If you would like to read about the prayer of *Examen*, I suggest *Sleeping with Bread: Holding What Gives You Life*, by Dennis Linn, Sheila Fabricant Linn, and Matthew Linn.

Journaling

You will notice, as you read on, that I suggest you journal the outcome of what God has been speaking to you. It can be good to make a note of how God speaks to you as you reflect on scripture, and what he is doing within you, so you do not forget. For the *Examen*, you might write the date as a heading, and a highlight and a lowlight of your life for each day. You might want to write about what you feel each day and notice those times when you feel consoled, or desolate, where you have felt God is distant. You do not need to write a lengthy essay of the outcome of your time with God. It might be a few words or even one word, or you may have a picture in mind to draw.

You may already have a journal you write or draw in, but if not, it is worth purchasing a small exercise book. It can either have lines or not, whatever your preference. These are your private writings so you will want to be as honest as you can. You are writing your journal in the presence of Jesus, and you are the only person who will read these notes. You might want to address your writings to God or Jesus or just write for yourself. You might have dreams you want to write down and remember. Remember to write about your struggles, along with what you see as spiritual things. It can be helpful to return to these writings at the end of an extended period, like a year, and reflect again on the journey of your life. If you practice this, you will notice and explore your relationship with God.

Conclusion
I hope and pray these contemplations, and the scriptures, poems and reflections which accompany them, will feed and nourish you. May God bless you richly as you go through each day.

Day 1

Before Creation

Contemplation

Before the world began; before heaven and earth, light and darkness, sea, sky, and land; before flowers flourished and bore fruit, or the moon and stars glowed; before the sun beamed its heat upon all living creatures that would dwell on the earth, God was alive and in love.

The One, whom we know as Father, Son, and Holy Spirit, always has and will live in a loving, harmonious, unified, peaceful, wondrous, gracious, and beautiful relationship. "God is love".[12] If God were singular, he could not be love, as love involves a loving relationship with another person. The American theologian, Robert E. Webber, coined the phrase "God's incarnational embrace",[13] to emphasise this inseparable communion between Father, Son, and Holy Spirit. Although distinct in their own personhood, so entwined is their relationship that not one person does anything without the other. They do everything together in love. God never needed humanity to fulfil him, but out of overflowing love, and because Father, Son, and Holy Spirit are eternally relational, we were invited into his "incarnational embrace."

Out of love and relationship, God desired to share himself with humanity and invite us into his loving relationship. He created humankind in his image, which meant the freedom to have choices, to reign and to rule, and be creative with everything given to us. We were created to love and have relationships, firstly with the One who created us in love, and secondly to love and have relationships with all of humanity. God, who is loving, relational, overflowing with grace and beauty, who cares for and looks after creation with joy and desire, created humankind in his image.

Reflection

Consider the God of love in Father, Son, and Holy Spirit and reflect on who he is. Take time to wander outside or sit in silence, play music, or lie on the grass and gaze at the sky. Reflect on moments that come to mind where you have experienced God's presence, and dwell on his goodness in your life history. Talk with him as you would with a deeply loved friend. Journal what God has spoken to you after you have spent time with him.

Practical

Centering Prayer is a centuries-old practice which opens us to the presence of God within us. It can be done several times a day. You could start by practising this for five minutes, and then over the days build up the time until you are engaging with this practice for longer, up to twenty minutes. The aim as you practise Centering Prayer is to rest in God and his loving presence and sit with him. The following guide to this practice is from the contemplative theologian and author, Father Thomas Keating.

Practice of Centering Prayer[14]

1. Choose a sacred word such as Abba, Father, Jesus, Spirit, love, peace etc. You can ask Jesus for a word that is specific to you at this time.
2. Sit in a comfortable, quiet place. Close your eyes. Breathe in and out, noticing your breath. Introduce the word into your mind and reflect on the word as you breathe in and as you breathe out. You are inviting the presence of God into your life and opening yourself to him.
3. If distractions occur, gently unite yourself with the word and so with God's presence, who longs to be with you.
4. At the end of the prayer time keep silent and with your eyes closed for a few minutes.
5. You have spent precious time in God's presence. Stand up and stretch and carry on with your life.

Scripture

Another form of praying is *Lectio Divina*. This prayer practice invites reflection on a portion of scripture. Slowly read the scripture and stop when a verse or word speaks to you and stay with that word or verse and let God speak to you through it. When you are ready, move on with the passage and stop again when another word or phrase speaks to you.

Today the scripture is Psalm 103. Before you start the prayer time, settle into God's presence by sitting in a comfortable position and consider how God, your Father, is looking at you with great love and acceptance. Then slowly read the psalm; savour each verse, allowing Holy Spirit to guide you and speak to you as you reflect on the passage. You may choose to reflect on only a few words or phrases within this psalm, or if you have more time, you may choose to ponder on more. The main aim is that this nourishes you and you spend time with God. After you have finished the meditation, you may like to journal what Holy Spirit has been saying to you.

Poem

A poem you might like to reflect on as you rest in God's presence and allow God to love you is "Let your God love you" by Edwina Gateley.

Examen

During the day or evening, reflect on the day and consider when you felt close to God and when you felt distant from God or sad. Offer these moments to God in prayer and thankfulness that you can talk to him, and he listens. Write in your journal and include what Holy Spirit is saying to you.

Day 2

Created in Love

Contemplation

"In the beginning" we read that "God created the heavens and the earth"[15] and the Holy Spirit hovered over the waters. In John's gospel, we read that from the beginning God's Son was the Word with God and was God.[16] The Father created all this world as we know it, with his Son and Holy Spirit. Everything that God spoke into being "was very good"[17] and is still very good. The heavens, the earth, the waters, the air we breathe, the plants and animals, light and darkness, the moon, sun, and stars were all created before us and for us. They were made so we could live and enjoy life in its fullness, and everything that God made was "very good" and had a purpose.

After God had created all that humanity needed to live and thrive, he created man and woman in his image, a gift to his Son, Jesus Christ.[18] God created humanity "to live in union with himself".[19] God embraced us from the very beginning because he always wanted to be with us. God's wanting to be with us is the reason we were made, and we are a beautiful image of God's amazing love. God loves and cares for all that he has made, which is why he invited us to participate with him to live a life overflowing with life's riches as we fulfil his purpose with him. As every plant and animal has a purpose, so we too have a purpose, but we get to share our purpose with God's purpose for us.

Firstly, we were made to love and be in a relationship with the One who created us. We call this worship. Our being in love and relationship with God makes us like him as we absorb and reflect his goodness. The more time we spend with God, the more we become like him. King David said: "One thing have I asked of the Lord, that will I seek after: that I may dwell in the house of the Lord all the days of my life, to gaze upon the beauty of the Lord…"[20] Secondly, we were each given gifts by our loving Father to partner with him in all

26

we do. This was never meant to be a burden, but a wonderful expression of who we are and how we are made. As God is creative, so we are creative. Living with him and serving him in doing his will is the most extraordinary and life-giving existence anyone can ever be involved in.

In our being united to Father through Jesus Christ by Holy Spirit, our spiritual life is nourished "through the contemplation on the mysteries of God and participation in the life of God through the doing of God's purposes".[21] As we contemplate all creation, and see God's beauty and love in animals, insects, plants, and his word, he opens our minds and hearts to understanding. This leads us to desire and even more participate in all he has for us, and so his purpose is revealed and in wonder and love, we join him in our vocations. This loving embrace in unity and purpose is the living breath that propels us, his body, to action.

Reflection
Ask God to show you how he loves and cares for you and how he has lovingly created you. You are a gift to his Son. Receive this truth.

Practical
Take a walk outside and ask God to show you who he is through the beauty of nature. Talk with Jesus as you would with a dearly loved friend and thank him.

Scripture
The scripture for today is Ephesians 2:4-10. Before you start this *Lectio Divina* prayer time, spend a few minutes considering how God, your Father, is looking at you with great love and acceptance. Then, slowly read the scripture. Savour each word and verse, allowing Holy Spirit to guide you and speak to you as you reflect on the passage. Journal after you have finished the meditation.

Poem
St. Hildegard of Bingen was a multi-talented Benedictine abbess and mystic of German descent who died in the 12th century. You may like to reflect on her poem which starts:
"I am the one whose praise

Echoes on high…"

Examen

During the day or evening, reflect on your experience with God. Reflect on when you felt moved towards God and his love, and when you felt distant from him, which resulted in you feeling sad or uncomfortable. Offer these moments to God in prayer and thank him that you can talk to him, and he listens. Journal the outcome.

If you have children, you may like to reflect on the day together. You could light a candle and share about your day around the table when you have your evening meal. The children can share when they received joy or sadness or what were the highlights or lowlights of their day. You can listen to your children share and share your feelings and when you felt drawn to God's presence and delight or saddened or drawn from his presence. You can together thank Jesus for your day and for the joy of good things that he has given to you.

Day 3

God Loves Us

Contemplation

Everything that God created was good, made as gifts for us and out of love for us. God created and gifted us, his creation, to enable us to know him and live in love with him. So much expression in the Bible comes from the authors seeing and experiencing God within nature. Their response was often one of praise and worship as they looked at God's creation and all that he had given to them. We too are stewards or gardeners of God's creation. We show our love to God through acceptance of the gifts he has given us, and we partner with him in caring for these gifts. God's most beautiful creation is humanity and our love for God deepens as we love and care for one another. As we long to love God and know him, we do what we call worship or prayer.

Prayer is "the central avenue God uses to transform us".[22] But prayer is difficult because it requires us to take our focus off ourselves and everything around us and be attentive to God over the distractions of the world. It requires us to be honest with ourselves and to trust the One who knows us better than we know ourselves. "Worship ushers us into the transforming presence of God".[23] In fact, God made us to worship, and we are not able to not worship because that is how we are created. "The issue is not whether we will worship but what we will worship".[24] Worship is not about singing songs, or sitting in silence, but being transformed by Christ's presence within us as our spirit unites with Holy Spirit. If we have not been transformed by worship, then we have not been in worship.

When our focus is not on God, we make ourselves the focus. Rather than see others as loved creatures, created in God's image, we see and treat them as lesser beings. When we misuse people, it affects our loving relationship with God and our growth as loving people.

We misuse God's gifts to us, and rather than a gift they become an obstacle or barrier in our relationship with God. All that God gifts to us are treasures to be cared for and valued. Whether these gifts are people, possessions, or something else, we accept them lovingly and gratefully, knowing they come from God in whom we trust.

Let us fix our eyes on Jesus and choose to desire him, because we do have a choice. He has chosen us,[25] and we have a choice to wholeheartedly choose him and his life for us or go our own way. Tell him again that you desire him because he loves to hear this. Choose to desire Jesus over everything else. You might like to offer him your health or your sickness, your riches or your poverty, your success, or your failure, your long or short life, and surrender this all to Jesus Christ, because he loves and desires us more than we could even imagine.

Reflection
What gifts has God given you? Do you see these gifts as gifts from God to be used for his glory, or are you so attached to the gifts that you seek the gift, rather than the Father who gave them to you? Surrender your gifts to Jesus in prayer and ask him to give you the deep desire of his heart for you. Pray for God's gift and grace to help you see others with his love.

Practical
As God loves you and created you, you might like to create and love a plant. If you are reading this in the spring season, you might like to sow a sunflower seed and, over these weeks, watch it germinate and grow (or not), and notice what you experience within you as you contemplate this creation. God may speak to you as you watch the sunflower germinate and grow. You may want to create something else! If you have children, you might like to involve them.

Scripture
The scripture for *Lectio Divina* this day is Ephesians 1:3-14. Before you begin the prayer time, seat yourself in a comfortable position and for a few minutes consider how God, your Father, is looking at you with great love and acceptance. Ask Jesus for a deep awareness of his love and a growing sense of how he gifts you. Ask Jesus to help you

desire to surrender yourself to him and to respond with generosity and all your heart to his love. Slowly read the scripture. Savour each verse, allowing Holy Spirit to guide you and speak to you as you reflect on the passage. Journal after you have finished the meditation.

Poem

The poem "Fall in Love" was written by Joseph Whelan S.J., but made famous by Pedro Arrupe, S.J., and often attributed to him. It is a beautiful poem which reveals how being in love with God affects our whole life.

Examen

During the day or evening, reflect on your experience with God and when you felt moved towards God and his love, maybe through someone or something. Note when you felt distant from him, sad, or uncomfortable, or even irritated by someone or something. Offer these moments to God in prayer and thankfulness that you can talk to him, and he listens. Journal these experiences and what Holy Spirit is saying to you.

If you have children, you may like to reflect on the day together. You could light a candle and share about your day around the table when you have your evening meal. The children can share when they received joy or sadness or what were the highlights or lowlights of their day. You can listen to your children and then share your feelings. Share when you felt drawn to God's presence, and when you felt saddened, irritated, uncomfortable or drawn from his presence. You can together thank Jesus for your day and for the joy of good things that he has given to you.

Day 4

Dreams and Desires

Contemplation

Much of the contemplation for today is taken from a book called *God of Surprises* by the Scottish Jesuit priest, Gerard W. Hughes S.J., who died in 2014. I refer to a chapter in this book entitled "General Directions for Digging".[26]

In this chapter, Hughes refers to a host who prepares a meal and has guests over to share the food. He asks whether our preference would be for a guest to pick over the food, hardly eating anything, but proclaiming that the food is delicious, or for the guest to devour the food "like a hungry dog" and ask for more. Likewise, if our praise is not genuine then it is not praise but "empty flattery".

St. Ignatius of Loyola (1491-1556) states that the
> human person is created to praise, reverence and serve
> God our Lord, and by so doing save his soul or her soul;
> and it is for the human person that the other things on
> the face of the earth are created, as helps to the pursuit
> of this end.[27]

In this context, Hughes suggests that the soul is the deepest part of ourselves, which incorporates all that we are. The soul is involved in everything we experience, whether we are aware of it or not. All our desires, "hopes, fears and anxieties, restlessness and ambition are expressions" of our soul.

St. Augustine of Hippo (c. 354-430 AD) was a theologian and philosopher from North Africa. He praised God, saying: "You made us for Yourself and our hearts are restless until they find rest in You".[28] The deepest part of our being will always be restless unless we are moving completely towards God. The indication that we are trying to satisfy ourselves, rather than live for God, is that we feel empty and bored or frustrated and dissatisfied with what we are doing. In our frustration and dissatisfaction, we will then give ourselves to something else, and the same thing will happen again because we are trying to satisfy ourselves. The negative feelings of sadness, anxiety, boredom, or frustration are expressions of our soul declaring we are living the wrong life. If we ignore the negative feelings, we can end up taking a wrong turn in life, but if we notice them, we can do something about them.

Paul the apostle writes, there is nothing in all creation that cannot lead us into the presence of God. Even the evil, that seeks "to separate us from the love of God in Christ Jesus our Lord",[29] can draw us into God's presence.

Hughes continues the chapter by uncovering what St. Ignatius meant when he talked about indifference or detachment. This term describes a person who is so connected to God that there is nothing in life that the person would not readily let go if God should ask them to do so. It is not about squashing desires a person has, but the person is living a life so fully present to God, that everything the person does or owns is secondary to the One who is the giver of the gift. We can discover God through our relationships with those around us and by living in the world. As a human being created in the image of God who is love and is relational, we need relationships and love. As we receive and give love, we come to know God.

To know God and love him more deeply, we need to let go of that which leads us away from God and choose that which leads us towards God. Finding our true God-given desires and what give us life is like finding treasure hidden in the field of ourselves. God will lead us to search for this treasure and discover it. We experience conflict as we try to follow our own desires and do what we want, but so often we are not sure what our own desires really are. When we find that treasure of our deepest desire that God has placed within us, then we discover what God's will is for our life. Hughes notes that the mid-life crisis can be that point in life when a person discovers they have been doing something for years that does not give them life. The person then tries to discover what will give them life.

The reason we find it so hard to live according to God's will is that we have an internal struggle going on within us. We want creation to praise, reverence and serve ourselves and we put ourselves before God. We want to receive the praise for what we do, rather than recognise that we can do nothing without God who gifts and guides us. It is his will, not ours, that is done on earth as in heaven.[30] When a person discovers the treasure of that deep desire that God has placed within them, then they live according to God's will, and it brings peace and harmony to their life. You will notice these people because they live in freedom and joy in the peace of Christ, even in suffering.

Reflection and Practical

Take a page in your journal and divide it into two columns. In one column write events which give you life and joy, and in the other column write about what drains you of life. Do you notice any events or attachments which are destructive to you and any which are creative and draw you into God's presence? You can use this to discern where God is guiding you as he is life and gives life. He desires for you to live in his presence in all you are and all you do.

Poem

R. S. Thomas was a Welsh poet and Anglican priest who died in 2000. His poem, "The Bright Field", describes the value of the treasure in the field of our innermost being.

Examen

During the day or evening, reflect on your experience with God and when you felt moved towards God and his love, maybe through someone or something. Note when you felt distant from him, saddened or uncomfortable, or even irritated by someone or something. Offer these moments to God in prayer and thankfulness that you can talk to him, and he listens. Journal these experiences and what Holy Spirit is saying to you.

If you have children, you may like to reflect on the day together. You could light a candle and share about your day around the table when you have your evening meal. The children can share when they received joy or sadness or what were the highlights or lowlights of their day. You can listen to your children and then share your feelings. Share when you felt drawn to God's presence, and when you felt saddened, irritated, uncomfortable or drawn from his presence. You can together thank Jesus for your day and for the joy of good things that he has given to you.

Day 5

Ugliness and Disorder

Contemplation

God created everything that humankind needed to thrive and live a beautiful life. Afterwards, he made man and woman, who entered this beautiful paradise to gaze on and experience all that had been gifted to them. As soon as they were created, they entered into the seventh day, which God had made "holy, because on it God rested from all his work that he had done in creation".[31] "God rested to let the world he had made flourish as it should. He rested in order to delight in its flourishing".[32] Adam and Eve were gifted with entering God's rest with him and delight in seeing the creation around them flourish. But we know the story. We turned away from God and believed in a lie that we could follow our own desires and they would be more fruitful than being with God, and disaster struck. It is not easy to reflect on the world, but that is what you are doing today. Do keep in mind as you pray and rest in God's presence that he is looking at you with great love.

This beautiful world which God created is not a happy, united, peaceful place, but is filled with unrest, disunity, and sadness. This is a result of sin and evil in the world. As we reflect on sin, it is not to think of our own personal sin, but the sin of the world into which we were born. We entered a world of sin when we were born, and whether we like it or not, we are a part of this sin.

There are wars waging that are prominent in our minds in many areas in the world, close to home and further away. There is always war somewhere on earth. There are people dying of hunger because there is nothing to eat where they live. In other parts of the world, fields of crops and unwanted food are thrown away. We might eat delicious food while we watch the news about people dying in war or dying of starvation. Children who are victims of violence and abuse can grow up and become the violent abuser of their childhood. Greed rules across the world, where the minority seek power and worldly riches, with a modest regard to ease the pain and suffering of those who have little. We live in a world of hate, disunity, racism, rape, and selfishness. Disease invades our friends and family and our land. We can be a victim of sin and we can be a source of sin.

We discard rubbish around the countryside which pollutes the ground and kills our creatures. We create mountains of garbage which we do not want to keep in our country, so we ship it off to pollute a distant land. We love our plastic because it is so useful, and our oil keeps our homes warm and the showers hot. We destroy the sea creatures with what we toss out, whether intentionally or through negligence. We love our phones and storing photos and the wonder of technology, and the cloud which is so useful for keeping everything. We do not consider the enormous amount of water needed for online messaging, which is depleting reservoirs in the world. We eat God's loved creatures whose sole existence has been to create food with no thought for their well-being. Factory farms provide cheap meat, eggs and milk from creatures who never go outside to see the environment they were created to live in. Our health, along with that of the animal, is endangered because of this practice and the countryside suffers as land is given up for something more profitable.

> When sin enters the story, shalom is vandalized. God's glorious intention for his good creation is subverted. The wholeness and harmony we were created to enjoy with God, with each other, with creation and with ourselves is fundamentally violated.[33]

We might not personally think we have anything to do with the sin and evil happening in the world, but in some small way we all play our part. As we pray today, we do not pray to understand why there is all this sin and evil, but we pray for God's grace to feel and see the sin and experience God's love and compassion for the world.

Reflection

Ask Jesus to gift you with the grace to feel the sin of the world and experience his love and compassion for this place we live. This might not be pleasant or easy to reflect on but stay with it if you can, so you can begin to glimpse the world as God sees it. You might like to go for a walk while you reflect or sit quietly. Consider all that God has made and what sin and people have done to his creation. Talk with Jesus about this as you would with a friend. Journal the outcome.

Scripture

Today you are invited to contemplate on scripture using the method of *Imaginative Prayer*. Choose one of the two suggested scriptures. In *Imaginative Prayer* you read the scripture several times until you have the story in your mind, then put the scripture aside and reflect on the story in your mind. Play the story back as you enter the scene. Imagine yourself there as a character in what is going on. You might smell, taste, see what is happening in the story as you imagine yourself being there. Who are you? The scriptures to choose from are the rebellion of Adam and Eve in Genesis 3:1-13 or Mark 6:17-29 about the beheading of John the Baptist.

Before you start reading consider how God is looking at you with great love. Pray for God's grace that as you enter the passage you would feel the sin of the world and experience God's love and compassion for it. Read the passage several times, letting the scene sink into your mind until you can set the Bible aside and enter the scene with your imagination as to what is happening. Reflect on what is happening as you imagine yourself there. Maybe you are Adam or Eve or a bystander. Maybe you are a guest at Herod's banquet. This type of prayer is not to judge the event or to study the words but to be there. You may want to talk to God at some point during your prayer time. When your prayer time comes to an end, do talk to God about your experience, and thank him for what he is doing within you. Journal the outcome.

Examen

During the day or evening, reflect on the day and consider what drew you close to God and what distanced you from God. Did you sense you were feeling what God was feeling about the sin of the world? Offer these moments to God in prayer and thankfulness that you can talk to him, and he listens. Journal the outcome.

If you have children, you may like to do this time of reflection together. You could light a candle and share around the table when you have your evening meal.

Day 6

Our Part in Sin

Contemplation

Shalom is a Hebrew word, and means the state of peace, wholeness, completeness, stillness, and harmony in which Jesus desires us to rest. Whenever we are drawn away from God, we can experience dis-ease, stress, or dissatisfaction, or feel hurried with the pace of life. If we notice this, we can take steps to still ourselves and focus once again on God and enter his presence. Shalom is what life is supposed to be like.

On day 5 we looked honestly at sin and evil in the world. We sin and we are also victims of sin. There are forces that conspire against shalom and these are the world, the flesh, and the devil. When faced with a situation we find hard, without God we try to disengage, which leads to control in our effort to cope and avoid the painful and chaotic reality. If we can escape from reality, we hope to numb ourselves to the pain we are in. But it does not go away. If we disengage from the brokenness in our lives, we might hit a place where we become completely overwhelmed. "Despair comes when our sense of control is lost and our attempts at escape leave us empty … We lose the capacity to dream of a better future".[34] I hope this is not you. If it is, please talk to someone who can help you.

Today pray for God's grace for intense sorrow for your sin. Pray to Jesus to ask him what he desires to show you and ask him for his gift to experience sorrow for sin. Sorrow is not guilt, so please do not feel guilty. Ask Jesus to guide you.

The following is a prayerful meditation on sin. This exercise may be hard, so do be gentle on yourself as Jesus is gentle on you. You may want to journal the outcome.

1. Prayerfully reflect on your life and allow Christ to bring up any area of sin as you revisit your past from your childhood

to your growing up to where you are now. If Christ brings something to mind, ask him what was in your heart at that time.

2.   Reflect on the ugliness of the sin and consider whether you are more valuable than those around you that you needed to have your own way in this sin.

3.   Consider how God knows everything about you. Before a word is on your lips, he knows.[35] He is the one who loves you, who gives you good desires and who shapes you into his likeness which leads to you loving people along with happiness. You are free to go your own way and do your own thing and Jesus respects that. He is gentle and patient, never gives up on you as he loves you and always desires a relationship even when you do not. Reflect on the truth of who you are and thank Jesus that he gives you life, supports and cares for you. Thank Jesus for anything else that comes to mind.

4.   Reflect on creation and the ordered universe. The oxygen that gives us breath and life, the flowers that bloom in beauty and the birds that sing, the sun that shines warmth and the moon and the stars that light up the sky. Are you grateful for creation and all the beauty God gives to you?

Reflection

Reflect on your own life and consider what you have done for Christ, what you are doing for Christ and what you will do for Christ. Talk with Jesus as you would chat with a friend and listen to him talking to you. Journal the outcome.

Scripture

The scripture for *Lectio Divina* today is Psalm 51 and the words of David. Before you start this prayer time, consider how God, your Father, is looking at you with great love and acceptance. Ask Jesus in prayer for his gift that you might experience intense sorrow for sin as you contemplate. Slowly read the scripture. Savour each verse, allowing Holy Spirit to guide you and speak to you as you reflect on the passage. You may be drawn to reflect on the whole psalm, or you may be drawn to a few words or verses.

At the end of your prayer time talk with Jesus, as with a friend, and pour out your thoughts and feelings to him. Thank him for who he is and how he is the One who gives life. You may want to be set free from feelings of sins of the past. In Christ, you are forgiven. You might want to say the Lord's prayer. Journal after you have finished the meditation.

Poem
Wendell Berry is an American novelist, poet, environmental activist, and farmer. Read and rest in the words of his poem entitled "The Peace of Wild Things".

Examen
During the day or evening, reflect on when you felt moved towards God and his love, and when you felt distant from him, which resulted in you feeling sad or uncomfortable. Offer these moments to God in prayer and thankfulness that you can talk to him, and he listens. You can also do this reflection with your children. Journal the outcome.

Day 7

Loved, despite Sin

Contemplation

Shalom is the state of peace, wholeness, completeness, stillness, and harmony in which Jesus desires us to rest. Shalom was what life was meant to be like. Consider Adam and Eve, whose lives were shattered beyond recognition by the simple act of picking a piece of fruit. Sadly, we did not trust God or believe in his goodness; we rebelled because we listened to a lie, broke our union with God, and all creation and humanity fell to sin and death. In our rebellion we are filled with greed, lust, and violence, as we focus on our own choices, trying to work out our own salvation to find happiness. As Adam and Eve sat in despair, outside their temple garden, I wonder whether they pondered on their past joy in the garden, and whether they experienced shalom through their reflection. I wonder, as they experienced the sorrow and sadness of their sin, whether they also experienced God's mercy and love for them. Today in prayer, we move from asking God to feel the sorrow and sadness of sin to reflecting on God's love and mercy on us, despite the sin.

Sin is like ivy or brambles which take over and swamp other plants or buildings. Ivy is beneficial to wildlife and a shelter for birds and small mammals, but it is immensely destructive and can cause great damage to buildings if left to roam. Its aerial roots, which line every stem, invade every crack and crevice of a wall, and penetrate every gap, tear apart the brickwork. It can cause buildings to look ugly along with the damage. When ivy is removed it still leaves its mark, and much scrubbing is needed to get rid of roots stuck in the brickwork. Such is the effect that sin can have upon our life. It wants to get into every crevice and seep into our minds and souls and impact our life and existence. It is only the sanctifying blood of Jesus Christ that cleanses, heals, and restores us, gently removing sin and its mark, and restoring us in love.

You may reflect and mourn about times you have turned away from God and desired to do your own thing. Is ingratitude an attribute you have adopted as you take so much for granted, or do you lack the desire to pray and spend time with Jesus? Do you lack hope that your life has any meaning? Today reflect on God's great love and mercy for you.

Reflection

Reflect on how loved you are in Christ and how he longs to be the centre of your life. Walk in the garden and consider the beauty of all that he has made and all he made for you. Feel the sun or the rain, listen to the birds, look at a bird or a single flower, or a cloud. Let Jesus guide you to a place where you can be with him. He is the source of all our life and love. Talk with him about what is going on in your life. Tell Jesus about your doubts and fears as you would chat with a friend and listen to him talking to you. Ask Jesus how he wants to love you. Ask Jesus what you can do to let him know you. Journal the outcome.

Poem

Denise Levertov was born in Britain and moved to America. She was a 20th century poet who authored many poems with religious themes. Can you "float into Creator Spirit's deep embrace" as you reflect on her poem, "The Avowal"?

Scripture

The scripture for *Lectio Divina* is Psalm 23, and you might want to reflect at the end of the day. Before you enter prayer, consider how God looks at you with love. Then in prayer, ask him for his great love and mercy as you reflect and pray. Slowly read the scripture. Savour each verse, allowing Holy Spirit to guide you and speak to you as you reflect on the passage. At the end of your prayer time talk with Jesus, as with a dearly loved friend. Thank him for who he is and how he is the One who gives you life. Journal the outcome.

Examen

During the day or evening, reflect on when you felt moved towards

God and his love, and when you felt distant from him, which resulted in you feeling sad or uncomfortable. Offer these moments to God in prayer and thankfulness that you can talk to him, and he listens. Journal the outcome.

If you have children, you may like to do this time of reflection together. You could light a candle and share around the table when you have your evening meal.

Day 8

Where am I?

Contemplation

Where are you? What have you noticed going on within you as you go through these contemplations on Christ and creation? Have you fulfilled each daily contemplation? Was your initial desire to fulfil each daily contemplation, but this has not happened as planned, as other activities have taken place? Have you just opened this book, and this is the first contemplation you are reading and about to engage with? If this is you, "welcome". This is the day to consider where you are and how you are experiencing the contemplations.

You may or may not be engaging with the *Examen* as a tool to contemplate on your life and walk with Christ. The former soldier and founder of the Society of Jesus (Jesuits), St. Ignatius of Loyola, recommended that all his pilgrims engaged with the *Examen*. He insisted that this simple exercise of reflecting on what I am most grateful for and what I am least grateful for, was exercised several times a day. The *Examen* changed St. Ignatius from a wild soldier to a pilgrim walking barefoot to Jerusalem. He expected God to speak through his deepest feelings and yearnings which he called "consolation" and "desolation". For centuries, prayerful people have found direction in their day and life through identifying these moments. Ignatius acknowledged that the Bible is divine, but so also is life, and God is constantly revealing himself and talking to us in our life experiences. As the missionary branch of the Catholic church, Ignatius' pilgrims were understandably busy, and felt they were too busy to undertake the contemplation and prayer assigned to them. Ignatius saw the *Examen* as the cornerstone of spiritual life to the extent that when Jesuits asked if they could skip them as they did not have time, he advised them to skip anything but the *Examen*.

The *Examen* is often done at the end of the day, but it can be done at any time. The best practice is to do it at a time that is most beneficial to you and so serves you. If you are an early morning person, you might like to reflect on the previous day first thing in the morning when you wake up. You might like to do it at midday or midnight. You can reflect on a day, or on a year or on ten years. It can be done alone, or it can be done together with friends, colleagues, or a family. It is something you can do each day to discover who you are, and who others are, and what in life brings you consolation and what brings desolation and bring this in prayer to God. When done together you might discover that an event or situation that brings joy and thankfulness to one person, might have the opposite effect on another person. We are all wonderfully made with different gifts and enjoyments.

I used the *Examen* when I reflected on my years in gardening and my years working with a Christian mission organisation (Youth With A Mission (YWAM). The *Examen* brought me back to YWAM after a ten-year break, as I discerned those times of consolation and desolation working in gardening and the previous years of working in missions.

Ignatius suggested lighting a candle because he saw the candle's flame symbolising the light of divine revelation in our everyday experience. The gratitude questions are a simple way of discovering consolation and desolation, and the interior movements through which divine revelation unfolds.

Examen Reflection
Reflect on your experience of these contemplations so far. For what are you most thankful? For what are you least thankful? You may have wanted to spend more time with Christ but have realised that your preference has been to watch television, read a book, play games or be with family and friends. Do you notice a resistance to enter God's presence or a desire to rest in him? There is no judgement involved here, or any criticism or condemnation, but a quiet noticing and recognition of who we are that we bring before God, who knows everything. Consider this time since starting the contemplations and what you are grateful for and for what you are least grateful. What has brought you close to God and what has distanced you? Offer these moments to God in prayer and thankfulness that you can talk to him,

and he listens. Journal the outcome.

Scripture

Choose from either Luke 15:11-32, about the father who has two sons, or Luke 7:36-50, about the woman who washed Jesus' feet with her tears. Decide on which passage you will devote yourself before you start meditating.

The method for contemplation is *Imaginative Prayer*. Read the passage at least five times, taking in everything that is said so you can remember the scene. Then put the Bible aside and recall the story in your mind, entering the scene so you become part of the story. Who are you? You may be the woman who washes Jesus' feet, a bystander, or a Pharisee. You may be one of the sons or a servant in the father's house. What do you smell? What do you taste? What do you feel? What about the scenery and the people around you? Do you talk to someone? What conversation do you have? Are you just looking on? Do you see Jesus or the Father? What are they like? Do you talk to either of them? Imagine yourself in the story and spend at least 20 minutes and not more than 60 minutes in this kind of prayer. At the end talk with Holy Spirit about your experience and record your reflections in your journal.

Poem

Macrina Wiederkehr was a Benedictine sister who lived at St. Scholastica Monastery in Fort Smith, USA. She was a spiritual director, retreat director, and author of several books. She died in 2020. Her poem for today is called "The Sacrament of Letting Go".

Examen

Reflect on this day at a time that serves you and share your experience with God. What are you most grateful for and for what are you least grateful? When have you felt moved towards God in love and when have you felt distant from him, saddened or uncomfortable? Offer these moments to God in prayer and thankfulness that you can talk to him, and he listens. Journal the outcome.

If you have children, you may like to do this time of reflection together. You could light a candle and share around the table when you have your evening meal.

Day 9

Christ's Call

Contemplation

As we follow Christ and minister with him, he forms us. If we are not being formed by Christ, we are not ministering with him. We can live and do good works all our lives but that does not mean that we are following Christ and ministering with him. We might be amazingly gifted and skilled in what we do. We might be preachers or teachers, architects or artists, writers or farmers, politicians or historians, administrators, or cleaners: the list is endless. In all that we are and do, we know we follow and minister with Jesus Christ because we are with him as we go about our daily schedule. We think about Jesus and invite him into what we are doing and talk with him, listen to him, and as we do this, he is forming us, drawing us into his presence and we experience Holy Spirit within us. As I write today, I think, Lord Jesus, what can I say? What draws these believers reading this to follow and minister with you each day? "We all thirst, whether we know it or not, for the presence of God, the reign of God and the peace of God",[36] but do we realise or believe this?

Our spiritual formation and ministering with Christ impact the way we use and develop the skills and gifts he has given us. It is not what we do, but *how* we do and live which reflects who we are. When we include Christ in our life, his love ministers through us in what we do and this flows into the lives of others. When we spend time alone with Jesus, we can think it is selfish because we should be doing good and serving in other places, but our being with Christ, sensing his presence and not hurrying to the next task, brings peace and transformation. If we are not following and ministering with Christ in all we do, then we are in danger of living for ourselves or others, rather than ministering with Christ in service to others. Have you experienced or are you experiencing weariness of work you are doing for God? Might God be waiting for you to minister with him, rather than on your own? Are you aware of Holy Spirit's presence within you as you go about your daily routine? What does it mean for Jesus to be your dearest friend and love?

We live each day with challenges and there are spiritual powers which seek to draw us away from God and subtly tempt us from his presence. If we lean on our own strength and ability rather than God, we can end up pursuing a call with no need for God. When we do something that stretches us, when we know we are weak, when we think there is no way we can do this in our own strength, we will see God do something wonderful if we are following and ministering with him. Our enjoyment and fulfilment in the gifts and skills we receive are always second to the One who has gifted us. If we are skilled and gifted, it is quite easy to minister and work without God. If we are skilled and gifted in an area which is needed in serving others, it is extremely easy to minister and work without God and receive affirmation and encouragement from all those around us and feed from that. It is Holy Spirit who gives us life.[37] It is Holy Spirit who conforms us to the image of Jesus Christ.[38] It is Holy Spirit who empowers us to minister in the mission of Jesus to the glory of Jesus and become like Jesus.[39]

Reflection

Ask Jesus Christ for his grace so that you will not be deaf to his call on your life but ready and willing to do anything he desires. Reflect on the motives of why you are doing what you do. Is what you are doing transforming you in humility, and growing you in Christ or are you building yourself up? How do you know if you are following and ministering with Christ in all that you do? Where do life and fulfilment come from? Talk with Holy Spirit and listen to what he is saying to you. Journal the outcome of this reflection time.

Ask Jesus to teach you his ways, to feel as he feels, to teach you to be compassionate to those suffering, diseased or poor, and to show you how to love and look at people. Pray that you might live as Christ lived, dependent upon Holy Spirit who dwells within you. Ask him to teach you his way so that it becomes your way, so you become a true companion of Christ and companion to others. Journal the outcome.

Scripture
The scripture for *Lectio Divina* today is Romans 12. Before you enter prayer, consider how God looks at you with love. Accept God's loving gaze upon you and offer yourself to him. Think about Jesus as he accepted his Father's loving gaze on him as he went about his daily routine and travelled around his homeland. Slowly contemplate on this chapter, letting the words speak to you. At the end of your prayer time talk with Jesus, as with a dearly loved friend. Thank him for who he is and how he is the One who gives you life. Journal the outcome.

Poem
George Herbert was a poet and priest in the Church of England who died in 1633. His poems on religious themes are in a publication entitled *The Temple*. "The Call" is a poem and a hymn set to music by several composers.

Examen
Reflect on the day and your experience with God. For what are you most grateful? When did you experience Christ's life and feel moved towards God? For what are you least grateful? When did you feel a lack of life or distance from God, saddened or uncomfortable. Offer these moments to God in prayer and thankfulness that you can talk to him, and he listens. Journal the outcome.

If you have children, you may like to do the *Examen* together. You could light a candle and do the reflection when you have your evening meal, breakfast, or lunch. You could do the *Examen* spontaneously when talking with your children.

Day 10

Kingdom Power

Contemplation

Reflect on Genesis 11:1-9 and the tower of Babel. Here we see a group of people who all spoke the same language. They were skilled in architecture and building and decided to build a city and a tall tower. This was just the start of what they were able to do to glorify themselves. Now that they could build themselves a city, nothing would be impossible for them.

We all have power, and we are responsible for the power we have. We might think people have more power than us, but, for better or for worse, we all exercise power. We need to recognise this, so we can use our power in a beneficial way. The poor, the vulnerable, and those who think they have nothing may not feel they have power. It might be that the power they have they use in the wrong way. They may feel shame because of the power used over them and they, in turn, may seek to use their power to rule or control someone else. Jesus used his power and authority to speak against the power and authority of the Pharisees, and he used his power to bring love, joy, and healing to the most vulnerable and poor in society. Jesus had immense power, "but made himself nothing, taking the form of a servant," and "he humbled himself by becoming obedient to the point of death, even death on a cross".[40] We cannot get away from power, but we can recognise it and use it for the benefit and love of others.

Reflection

Ask Jesus to teach you his ways, to feel as he feels, to teach you to be compassionate to those suffering, diseased or poor, and to show you how to love and look at people. Pray that you might live as Christ lived, dependent upon Holy Spirit who dwells within you. Ask him to teach you his way so that it becomes your way, so you become a true companion of Christ and companion to others. Journal what Jesus speaks to you.

Where do you try to make a name for yourself? Do you recognise the power you have and where you exercise that power? Who are the people who exercise power over you? Reflect on the exercise of power you have and the exercise of power over you and your community and listen to what Jesus says to you. Journal the outcome.

Scripture

Today reflect on scripture using *Imaginative Prayer*. In *Imaginative Prayer* you read the scripture several times, until the story is retained in your mind, then put the scripture aside and reflect on the story in your mind. Play the story back as you reflect and imagine what is going on. You might smell, taste, see what is happening in the story and imagine yourself being there.

The passage is Mark 5:21-43. It includes the story of Jairus, the ruler of the synagogue, whose daughter was dying, combined with the woman who had been bleeding for twelve years. She "had suffered much under many physicians, and had spent all that she had, and was no better but rather grew worse".[41]

Before you start reading, consider how God is looking at you with great love. Pray for God's grace that as you enter the passage you would feel as Jesus feels, and feel his compassion for those suffering, diseased or poor, and show you how to love and look at people. Read the passage several times, letting the scene sink into your mind until you can set the Bible aside and enter the scene with your imagination. Reflect on what is happening as you imagine yourself there. Who are you? Are you one in the crowd, a disciple, Jairus or the lady in pain? What do you say, or do you not say anything? What do you do? What do you feel? Do you feel powerful or powerless? What does Jesus say?

At the end of your prayer time talk with Jesus, as with a dearly loved friend. Thank him for who he is and for his leading you in *Imaginative Prayer*. Journal the outcome.

Poem

Today is another poem by the poet and Anglican priest, R. S. Thomas. It is titled "The Kingdom".

Examen

Reflect on the day and your experience with God. For what are you most grateful? Did you experience Christ's life and feel moved towards God? For what are you least grateful? Did you feel a lack of life or distance from God, saddened or uncomfortable? Offer these moments to God in prayer and thankfulness that you can talk to him, and he listens. Journal the outcome.

If you have children, you may like to do the *Examen* together. You could light a candle and do the reflection when you have your evening meal, breakfast, or lunch. You could do the *Examen* spontaneously when talking with your children.

Day 11

Kingdom Reign

Contemplation, Reflection and Scripture

Today centres on the reign of God, and Jesus who carried this reign on earth. You will reflect on what Jesus was like as he walked on this earth. Follow the points laid out below.

1. Reflect and receive the Father's loving gaze on you and surrender yourself to him.
2. Reflect on Jesus receiving his Father's loving gaze as he travelled around Israel. Imagine Jesus in the countryside, towns and the synagogue and let your imagination take you on a journey with him.
3. Pray and ask God to help you to hear him and follow his call, and be excited to persevere in all circumstances, knowing Jesus is always with you.
4. Read Luke 10:1-20 about Jesus sending out 72 disciples. Imagine you are with the 72 disciples whom Jesus sent out to minister healing, etc. Maybe you are one of them or are you observing? What do you see in Jesus that inspires you to listen to and follow him? What does Jesus look like? How is he dressed? What is the tone of his voice and the look in his eyes as he speaks to you? What is happening that captures your attention and your soul? Do you want to be a follower of Jesus in all that he does and wherever he goes, whether there are joys, sorrows, victories, or failures? Do you think this would be an honour? Do you feel apprehensive?

At the end of your prayer time talk to Jesus as you would with a friend, offering your prayers and thoughts to him. What does he say to you? You might not know God's call on your life, but do you have the desire to accomplish whatever that call might be and do that with Jesus? Journal the outcome.

Practical

How is your sunflower - or creation, if you have sown another seed? God created plants. To survive they need light, water, and carbon dioxide, which is the breath we breathe out. In return, they gift us oxygen and beauty.

Poem

"The Kingdom" (author unknown)
> When you say
> YES
> to the Kingdom
> things once felt
> indispensable
> slip by.
> One by one
> (hardly noticeable at first)
> you see them
> slip away.
> All that you held on to,
>
> possessed,
> claimed,
> somehow
> disappears
> melts into
> another horizon
> whilst you are busy
> with the new.
> You do not notice,
> until,
> in panic,
> you feel
> a lonely
> scaring loss
> and look around
> afraid.

Yes,
Things have changed.
Suddenly,
you want to cry
aloud,
to reclaim
to re-possess,
to re-establish,
but, oh, you
feel so naked
and different.
The Kingdom,
Ah, yes,
The Kingdom claims all.

Examen

Reflect on the day and your experience with God. For what are you most grateful? Did you experience Christ's life and feel moved towards God? For what are you least grateful? Did you feel a lack of life or distance from God, saddened or uncomfortable? Offer these moments to God in prayer and thankfulness that you can talk to him, and he listens. Journal the outcome.

If you have children, you may like to do the *Examen* together. You could light a candle and do the reflection when you have your evening meal, breakfast, or lunch. You could do the *Examen* spontaneously when talking with your children.

Day 12

Incarnation

Contemplation

Today we look at the incarnation of Christ. As you enter prayer, consider, and reflect on the truth that God looks at you with great love. Father, Son, and Spirit look on the world, know everything and see all that goes on. Consider that creation is the Father's gift to his Son and the Son comes to reign on earth. The following is an excerpt from a sermon preached by St Augustine at Christmas time in A.D. 411 or 412. As you reflect on this sermon, consider what our Father felt as his Son was born into this world, where there is love, joy and laughter, but also death, suffering and destruction. Pray for a deep and intimate knowledge of Jesus so that you can love and follow him. Let Holy Spirit speak to you as you ponder on the words.

> Man's Maker was made man,
> that He, Ruler of the stars,
> might nurse at His mother's breasts;
> that the Bread might be hungry,
> the Fountain thirst,
> the Light sleep,
> the Way be tired from the journey;
> that the Truth might be accused by false witnesses,
> the Judge of the living and the dead be judged by a mortal judge,
> Justice be sentenced by the unjust,
> the Teacher be beaten with whips,
> the Vine be crowned with thorns,
> the Foundation be suspended on wood;
> that Strength might be made weak,
> that He who makes well might be wounded,
> that Life might die.
> He was made man to suffer these and similar undeserved

things for us, that He might free us who were undeserving; and He who on account of us endured such great evils, merited no evil, while we who through Him were so bountifully blessed, had no merits to show for such blessings. Therefore, because of all this, He who before all ages and without a beginning determined by days was the Son of God, saw fit in these latter days to be the Son of man; and He, who was born of the Father but not made by the Father, was made in the mother whom He had made, that He might sometime be born here on earth of her who could never have been anywhere except through Him ... He cried in the manger in wordless infancy - He, the Word, without whom all eloquence is mute.[42]

Reflection

Consider Father, Son, and Holy Spirit as distinct persons, who have always lived in a loving relationship together. They are so closely knit that they are One and yet they are three. Father created the world as a gift for his Son. Before the world was created, he desired for humanity to have a relationship with him, and for his Son to dwell always with those he created. He invited humanity into his loving relationship.

Consider that the Son of God, Jesus, was always going to be born into the world through a woman, being fully God and fully human, and so enter the world to be King of his people. Even if we had never sinned, God's desire was always to enter the world he created and dwell with his people. This is the astounding good news. What does Jesus want to share with you? Talk with Jesus as you would with a friend about this wondrous truth and thank him that he desires to be with you always.

Scripture

Today you reflect on scripture using *Imaginative Prayer*. In *Imaginative Prayer* you read the scripture several times until you have the story in your mind, then put the scripture aside and reflect on the story in your mind. Play the story back as you reflect and imagine what is going on. You might smell, taste, or see what is happening in the story, and imagine yourself being there. The Scripture is Luke 1:26-38.

Before you start reading, consider how God is looking at you with great love. Pray as you enter the passage that you would experience deep intimacy with Jesus and know his love for you and the world, and that you will love him, and follow him, and do all he desires with him. Read the passage several times, letting the scene sink into your mind until you can set the Bible aside and enter the scene with your imagination. Reflect on what is happening as you imagine yourself there. Who are you? Are you Mary? Are you Joseph? Are you a friend who Mary confides in or someone looking on at what is happening, or are you yourself? What do you say, or do you say nothing? What do you do? What do you feel?

At the end of your prayer time talk with Jesus, as with a dearly loved friend. Thank him for who he is and that he chose to come into this world to be with us. Journal the outcome.

Poem
Today is another poem by the poet Denise Levertov and its title is "Annunciation".

Examen
Reflect on the day and your experience with God. For what are you most grateful? Did you experience Christ's life and feel moved towards God? For what are you least grateful? Did you feel a lack of life or distance from God, saddened or uncomfortable? Offer these moments to God in prayer and thankfulness that you can talk to him, and he listens. Journal the outcome.

If you have children, you may like to do the *Examen* together. You could light a candle and do the reflection when you have your evening meal, breakfast, or lunch. You could do the *Examen* spontaneously when talking with your children.

Day 13

Nativity and Journey

Contemplation

Today we look at the birth of Christ, as a baby was born into the world who was fully God and fully human. Consider that the Father created the world as a gift to his Son, Jesus. Jesus was always going to be born into the world to dwell with his people; such is the overwhelming love of God. How could he not want to be with us and for us to be with him in every way we could? To be in Christ is an invitation to be fully human, as Jesus was and is. Jesus not only came to defeat death and sin and draw us into a relationship with himself, but he came to show us what it is to be a true human being, made in the image of God, and live as God intended. The writer, lecturer and Orthodox churchman Metropolitan Kallistos Ware confirms this when he states, "Even had there been no fall, God in his own limitless, outgoing love would still have chosen to identify himself with his creation by becoming man".[43] Although we cannot know for sure what would have happened had we not sinned, the truth that God is love and desired to dwell with us, certainly implies that this was always the case. God has always desired to dwell with humanity and be in communion with us. He has always desired for humanity to join with him in taking stewardship of the world. As we consider our Christian formation it can be good, not just to focus on the wonder of being forgiven and saved but focus on the daily sanctifying work of the Spirit who forms us because of love and desire for relationship.

Since the rebellion of Adam and Eve, the only way for humanity to be united once again in eternal life and love in the Trinitarian God, was for God to enter our sin and death, defeat this evil, and personally bring us back into this loving relationship. The Son of God, Jesus, was born by the seed of the Father, so he was fully divine. He was born in the 1st century to a young virgin called Mary, so he was fully human. This miraculous birth was a sign of Jesus' distinctiveness and pointed to his eternal heavenly Father as his origin. Jesus was not a new species. In his humanity he was born with all the weakness and vulnerability of any other human being. As Ware points out, as Jesus was born in the normal way from a human person, "the Incarnation did not involve the coming into being of a new person".[44] Jesus was born in Bethlehem, where the 9-month pregnant Mary had travelled from Nazareth, because the Roman Emperor occupying the area had levied a tax on the people of Israel. Joseph, her husband, was with her as they journeyed to the town of Bethlehem. Jesus needed someone to care for him and do everything for a small baby to survive in the world.

As Israel and his family moved to Egypt to escape death and famine several thousand years before Jesus, similarly Mary and Joseph carried the infant Jesus to Egypt to escape the slaughter of children by Herod. The Father entrusted his Son to a humble, lowly couple, who listened to him and trusted in him to guide them, and the Father had to trust them! Meanwhile, Herod was wielding his power, by killing every child, in his effort to remain powerful.

A few years later the family returned to live in Nazareth. The gospel of Luke points to Jesus' vocation, when as a baby he was presented at the temple. Simeon claimed Jesus as the light of the world and one who had come to save the people.

Scripture

Today you reflect on scripture using *Imaginative Prayer*. In *Imaginative Prayer* you read the scripture several times until you have the story in your mind, then put the scripture aside and reflect on the story in your mind. Play the story back as you reflect and imagine what is going on. Before you start reading, consider how God is looking at you with great love. Pray that as you enter the passage you would experience an intimate felt knowledge of Jesus, who has become human for us, so that we may love him more and follow him more closely. Be aware, as you pray, of your gift in being able to respond to God, and your limitations, such as when you experience resistance in prayer. You may not have been able to respond to Jesus and follow him, surrendering everything to him yet, and that is fine. The main thing is to be honest with him and yourself, as he knows everything about you. You will experience a deeper love of Jesus as you come to know him. You are praying to know the human Jesus who walked on this earth and know him as you reflect on scripture and creation, not just knowing about him. The more you know him, the more you will become like him. There are two passages, so you can choose either one. Choose which passage you want to meditate on before you start.

The first passage is Luke 2:1-14, the story of the nativity and birth of Christ. As you enter prayer with this passage, imagine you are there with Mary and Joseph waiting for the Messiah to be born. Do you watch Mary and Joseph on their journey as they travel to Bethlehem and hear them talking? Do you talk with them, and do you feel what they are going through? Jesus is born into a poor family and from there he will redeem the world. Let your imagination flow as you watch the event of the birth of Christ and what is going on.

The other passage you can reflect on is Matthew 2:13-18, the flight to Egypt. According to Luke, Mary and Joseph took Jesus to the temple where he was circumcised like every other Jewish boy. Simeon and Anna recognised him as "the Lord's Christ".[45] They praised God and blessed the child. Matthew does not mention this event, and Luke does not mention that soon afterwards the family, in fear for the child's life, flee to another country. What do you think is going on in this family's mind as they have to flee? What do they feel? What do you feel? Whichever scripture you pray, pray for an intimate felt knowledge of our Lord, who has become human for us, so that we may love him and those he loves, and follow him more closely. Allow him to lead you as you enter your chosen passage.

At the end of your prayer time talk with Jesus, as with a dearly loved friend. Thank him for who he is and that he chose to come into this world to be with us. Thank him for being with you. Journal the outcome.

Poem

The American-born writer, T. S. Eliot, is considered one of the greatest poets of the 20th Century. He wrote prose, plays and non-fiction. "The Journey of the Magi" ponders on the journey of the three wise men who visited Jesus at his birth.

Examen

Reflect on the day and your experience with God. For what are you most grateful? Did you experience Christ's life and feel moved towards God? For what are you least grateful? Did you feel a lack of life or distance from God, saddened or uncomfortable? Offer these moments to God in prayer and thankfulness that you can talk to him, and he listens. Journal the outcome.

If you have children, you may like to do the *Examen* together. You could light a candle and do the reflection when you have your evening meal, breakfast, or lunch. You could do the *Examen* spontaneously when talking with your children.

Day 14

Early Years

Contemplation

Jesus was subject to everything that Jewish boys in the 1st century went through. He was circumcised on the 8th day,[46] according to the Jewish custom. Before returning from Jerusalem to Galilee, Joseph and Mary did "everything required by the Law of the Lord".[47] Jesus was taught the scriptures, and he grew in knowledge of his heavenly Father. He learned to trust his parents, play with them and the other children, pray and understand the scriptures with them, and to love those around him. He learned how to grow up as a Jewish boy. When Jesus was twelve years old, his family lost him in Jerusalem on a visit to the Passover festival. After three days, his parents found him chatting with the teachers at the Temple, who were astonished at his understanding. Luke states "Jesus increased in wisdom and in stature and in favour with God and man".[48] In the Temple, Jesus relinquished childhood, breaking emotional ties with his mother and father. He did not intend to hurt his family, but at this early age, he knew his true Father and desired to know everything about him and to tell others what he knew.

Jesus lived an ordinary human existence. He was raised in a family with other children. He learned the family trade and for most of his life he worked in manual labour as a carpenter. Yet, in this, possibly, mundane existence, we learn that he dedicated time to understanding scripture and "he became strong, filled with wisdom".[49]

Jesus learned the scriptures and came to understand them fully. He became wise and recognised good from evil. He understood the ways of the world, and how the Temple was organised, and he discerned where those in authority were leading people away from his Father. He grew in his relationship with God, his Father, and with the people who shared his life. Jesus was recognised by those who knew him to be illegitimate, so he was possibly ostracised from an early age. He came from a poor family and humbly worked in labour. It seems this life of learning to know God in scripture and a routine job is something we can imitate, as we desire to grow in wisdom and understanding of God. It was only when Jesus had grown in years, in wisdom, and in an understanding of his identity and purpose for his life, that his life changed as Holy Spirit empowered him for his final three years.

Jesus, in his humanity, lived dependent upon his Father and all his Father had for him to do. He lived by Holy Spirit within him, in the same way that we can all live by Holy Spirit. His character was formed in the same way that our character can be formed, as Holy Spirit sanctifies us. All that Jesus did in terms of miracles and healing he did in the power of Holy Spirit. Jesus showed us how to live a fully human life with Holy Spirit and we can do the same.

Jesus showed us what the purposes of God are for this world, and he has invited us to live accordingly. I wonder what age he was when he saw himself as the suffering servant in Isaiah; the fulfilment of the Old Covenant, and the One to bring in a New Covenant. As a baby, he would not have known all this.

Scripture

Today you reflect on scripture using *Imaginative Prayer* as you contemplate on Jesus growing up. In *Imaginative Prayer* you read the scripture several times until you have the story in your mind, then put the scripture aside and reflect on the story in your mind. Play the story back as you reflect and imagine what is going on. Before you start reading, consider how God is looking at you with great love. Pray that as you enter the passage you would experience an intimate felt knowledge of Jesus, who has become human for you. Pray to know him more clearly so that you might love him more dearly, and love those he loves, and follow him more nearly day by day.

The passage today is Luke 2:41-50 which recalls when Jesus was twelve years old and stayed behind in Jerusalem after the Feast of the Passover. It is the only scripture we have of Jesus's childhood years. Pray that you would get to know and love Jesus as you reflect on this passage and that you will love those he loves and follow him. Imagine watching Jesus growing up; are you a bystander or a member of his family or a family friend, a mother, a father, or a childhood playmate? Reflect on Jesus as he grew up and the values he received, the simple life he led in Nazareth as he waited for God's call, or his listening to God. How did he play with his brothers, sisters, and friends? Did he watch his father working as a carpenter, learning the skills he would use in later life? Do you see him mourning the death of his father?

What about the metaphors he used in his preaching and teaching later in life? As a child, he watched farmers sow seeds and birds peck at the ground. He picked flowers in the fields, and he watched the vine growers prune their vines. He watched sheep grazing, and maybe he saw one that was lost. He rejoiced in all of creation. Reflect on what you think Jesus was doing in these early years. Watch him as he thought deeply and went through the transition from child to adult, seeing illness and pain, worshipping in the synagogue, and playing with friends. You may want to contemplate with the scripture, or you may want to pray with your imagination as Holy Spirit leads you through these years that we can only imagine. At the end of your prayer time talk with Jesus, as with a dearly loved friend. Thank him for who he is and that he chose to come into this world to be with us. Thank him for being with you. Journal the outcome.

Poem

Pierre Teilhard de Chardin, S.J. was a French Jesuit priest, scientist, theologian, philosopher, and writer, who died in the USA in 1955. His poem, "Patient Trust", encourages us to trust that God is doing something good in our lives, whatever we are going through. It can take time.

Examen

Reflect on the day and your experience with God. For what are you most grateful? Did you experience Christ's life and feel moved towards God? For what are you least grateful? Did you feel a lack of life or distance from God, saddened or uncomfortable? Offer these moments to God in prayer and thankfulness that you can talk to him, and he listens. Journal the outcome.

If you have children, you may like to do the *Examen* together. You could light a candle and do the reflection when you have your evening meal, breakfast, or lunch. You could do the *Examen* spontaneously when talking with your children.

Day 15

Leaving Home

Contemplation

When Jesus was around 29 to 30 years old, he left home and Galilee and went to the river Jordan where he was baptised by his cousin, John.[50] Something had happened in Jesus' spiritual growth which caused his Father to lead him to baptism and into his last three years of ministry. Did Jesus hear news of John baptising and know that this was the sign for him to leave home? Did Jesus know where he was going when he left Galilee, or did he just go, knowing his Father would direct him along the way? What might he have said to his family before leaving? What do you think was in Jesus' heart as he left? Did he pray? Who did he meet along the way? Jesus was always listening to his Father, and only did what he heard his Father say.[51]

Scripture

Today, enter *Imaginative Prayer* with the gospel passage, Matthew 3:13-17. Imagine being with Jesus as he travels to the river Jordan. Use all your senses as you smell the air, the grass, the dust, and the river. What do you see, taste, hear and feel? Do you watch Jesus or travel with him by his side, or are you at the river Jordan and see him arrive? What does he say to you? What do you say to him? Do you hear the voice from heaven which says, "'This is my beloved Son, with whom I am well pleased?'"[52] What do you feel?

In *Imaginative Prayer* you read the passage several times until you have the story in your mind, then put the scripture aside and reflect on the story in your mind. Play the story back as you reflect and imagine what is going on. Before you start reading, consider how God is looking at you with great love. Pray that as you enter the passage, Jesus would open your heart and mind to know him better, love him more fully, and follow him more closely. When you have finished your prayer time, talk to Jesus as you would with a dearly loved friend, and thank him for spending time with you. Journal the outcome.

Practical
As an alternative or addition to writing in your journal, you might want to draw a picture, take a photo, press a flower, or do a sculpture and take a photo of it to put in your journal. You may like to walk in the countryside as you imagine walking with Jesus to the river Jordan, or along a riverside.

Reflection
I wonder if you are tired of the contemplations at this stage and want to give up? Do you feel you are not making progress in your relationship with God? Are you are loving this time and looking forward to it each day? Keep note each day of your consolations, where you are aware of a deep presence of God in your life, and desolations where you notice resistance in prayer, distraction, or temptation to want to go your own way and not be with Jesus, or a diminished desire to be involved. Be aware of choices that come up which deter you from prayer. Be aware of choices and decisions that arise, discerning whether the choice or decision that you desire is also God's decision for you.

Poem
The 20th century poet, Mary Oliver, was inspired by the natural world, and this was reflected in her many poems filled with creation's wonder. "The Summer Day" captures Oliver's gaze on a grasshopper in a field on a warm summer's day.

Examen
During the day or evening, reflect on your experience with God. When were you aware of God's presence in your life today? Were you aware of his deep love for you as you reflected on Jesus in prayer? Were you aware of Jesus as you walked in creation and felt his touch? Do you feel tired or desolate, or do you feel sad? Do you find these prayer times hard, and do you want to give up? Do you feel Jesus is distant? Offer these moments of consolation and desolation to God in prayer and talk to Jesus who listens to every word you say, and who

longs for you to love him deeply as he loves you. Journal the outcome.

If you have children, you may like to do the *Examen* together. You could reflect on the day over a meal around the table or walk in the countryside and share any joy and sadness together.

Day 16

Two Ways of Living

Contemplation

Today, we look at ourselves and consider our lifestyle, and whether our desires come from above and are God's ways, or come from below, and are the ways of the world or Satan. The strategies of Satan lead us to desire riches and to be honoured in what we do, which leads to pride and arrogance. Jesus desires us to trust completely in him, regardless of whether we are financially rich or poor. We might not seek to be poor, but Jesus was poor. We might not seek to be foolish, but many thought Jesus was foolish. We might not desire to be simple and humble, but Jesus was all of these. We may be insulted or condemned by others, but Jesus taught us not to attack but to be humble and loving. Are we willing to gaze on Jesus and see his characteristics and be willing to choose his way over ours? Let us consider what it means to live by the power of Holy Spirit and what it looks like to live under the power of Satan and the world.

The authors of *The Way of the Dragon or the Way of the Lamb*, suggest:
"The way from above is power *from* God and power *for* God; it is a power known in our weakness and expressed in love. The other way of power, the way from below, seeks power from within and pursues power as an end in itself."[53]

Are you open to listening to and being guided by others, or do you resist and desire no intervention about what you do and how you live? The power from below entices us to be possessive of our money, our possessions, and our friends, and to be eager to serve ourselves in whatever way we can. We control what we have for fear of losing anything, and we want recognition in all we do, which feeds our sense of power and authority. The way of Jesus is to humble ourselves and to be open to guidance from others, knowing we need their honest and wise advice, as we do not know it all. We offer our skills and gifts to benefit others, even when no one notices. We do not need to be commended by people to feel worthy for what we do, because we serve Jesus, and our worth is in him alone. We are generous with our possessions, and we do not put our own expectations on our friends whom we love.

Do you find your worth in others' approval of yourself, and feel anxious or depressed if this does not happen? What about if you fail? Do you try and cover up any failure, or are you content to accept your failures and limitations, seeking to learn and be vulnerable, knowing you can admit your weaknesses and ask for help? Are you secure in who you are or in what you have? "For freedom Christ has set us free",[54] says the apostle Paul. When we live in Christ, we experience freedom from needing to achieve, or needing confirmation from others in all we do. We experience freedom from holding on to material possessions and freedom from grasping power in our work responsibilities. Freedom guides us to accept outcomes we might not choose but which we are able to relinquish without distress.

Pride is when I exaggerate the importance of who I am and place myself at the centre of my life, rather than Jesus Christ. I see the gifts I am given as mine, rather than gifts given by God for the good of the world and others. Those who follow Jesus are humble and open to Jesus' intervening in their lives. They realise the gifts they have are not theirs to possess but to serve others and contribute to society. They know their true worth and identity in Christ and they value others, knowing each person is cherished by God. Those who live according to the standard of the world may hinder another person's growth to get higher up the ladder. They see people as a threat to their success, and blame or shame others to promote themselves, or twist the truth so they are seen in a favourable light. We see so much of this if we watch the news or follow politics, but we also see this in the lives of Christians. If we do not submit completely to Jesus, we can have a fleshly desire for power and vision. We will grab what we see as God's call on our lives with worldly enthusiasm. It can look good, and it can look as if we are following Jesus. How do we know whether we are dependent on God, or just doing our own thing? When we live in Christ, we trust in him and delight when others succeed, or we see gifts in others that we appreciate. We encourage them and are willing to share our gifts with them.

Scripture

Now is your time to reflect on your life through *Lectio Divina*. The scripture is 2 Corinthians 4:7-12. Before you start, consider how God, your Father, is looking at you with great love and acceptance. Then slowly read through the scripture; savour each verse, allowing Holy Spirit to guide you and speak to you as you reflect on the passage. Stop when a verse or word speaks to you and stay with that word or verse, until you feel ready to move on. Journal what Holy Spirit has said to you after you finish the meditation.

In 2 Corinthians 4:7-12, Paul talked about being weak, so that Christ was strong, and then the power of God worked through him. How do you see this in your life and what do you do to cultivate this way of living? How do you resist temptation and the ways of the world, and submit in holiness to God?

Poem

The Belgian, May Sarton, moved to the USA with her family when she was 4 years old in 1916, to escape German occupation during WW1. She was a prolific writer of poetry, novels, and non-fiction in the 20th century. One of her many poems is called, "Now I become myself".

Examen

Reflect on when you felt moved towards God and his love, and when you felt distant from him, which resulted in you feeling sad or uncomfortable. Maybe you felt close to Christ in your weakness, or distant as you sensed arrogance rise within you. Maybe you felt filled with hope, or maybe you felt tired or sad. What are you most grateful for and what are you least grateful for this day? Offer these moments to God in prayer and thankfulness that you can talk to him, and he listens. Journal the outcome.

If you have children, you may like to do the *Examen* together.

Day 17

Discerning Vocation

Contemplation

Parker Palmer understands vocation "not as a goal to be achieved but as a gift to be received." He continues:

> Discovering vocation does not mean scrambling toward some prize just beyond my reach but accepting the treasure of true self I already possess. Vocation does not come from a voice "out there" calling me to become something I am not. It comes from a voice "in here" calling me to be the person I was born to be, to fulfill the original selfhood given me at birth by God.[55]

Accepting your vocation or mission in life can be more demanding than attempting to be someone else. What is life to you? It is good to reflect on what gives joy to your soul, what is life-giving to you, and whether you are living according to how God has made you. Who is your true self that God has so lovingly formed, and are you damaging this beautiful image of God by wearing a mask? Are you living a lie in the belief that you must work for God, or do you find fulfilment and peace in your vocation? "The deepest vocational question is not "What ought I do with my life?" It is the more elemental and demanding "Who am I?" What is my nature?"[56]

We discern our mission and our deepest calling by growing into who we are truly meant to be, rather than who we think we ought to be. We find joy in understanding our true self that Jesus delights in. We do not need to look for a job or vocation to express who we are, but we look within ourselves for what delights us and delights Christ and then we do what we do out of who we are. This is not unique to Christianity, but unique to every human being made in God's image. We see our weaknesses when we do something that we were not created to do. We see gates that close as an indication that God is

75

closing those gates when we trust God to show us the path ahead. Instead of worrying about what we think we have lost, we can pray, and enjoy the scenery on the path God is leading us along.

If I live out of a gift I do not possess, and it is not a gift given to me by God, it can be a false and dangerous gift. What I do can look loving, but it is loveless if it is done from my need to prove myself, rather than to care for others. It is arrogant and faithless, based on the mistaken notion that God has no way of channelling this gift to others, except through me. When I persist with a gift which I do not possess, I burn out. When I share a gift which is given by God, it will renew itself and me even if I give it all away.[57]

Reflection

God has given you gifts, which give abundant life to you and those with whom you share your gifts. Reflect on those gifts God has given you. How do you best love others with the gifts God has given you? What about the skills or gifts you received from your family and upbringing? How are you putting those gifts to use? Do you have God-given gifts that you are not using?

Practical

How is your sunflower? Is it alive? Does it need repotting? Consider whether Jesus is guiding you to be creative in other practical ways, such as drawing, painting, writing, gardening etc. and if this gives you life, start creating.

Scripture

Today, reflect on the scripture using *Imaginative Prayer*. In *Imaginative Prayer* you read the scripture several times until you have the story in your mind, then put the passage aside and reflect on the story in your mind. Play the story back as you reflect and imagine what is going on. You might smell, taste, see, hear, and touch what is happening in the story and imagine yourself being there. The scripture is Luke 4:1-13 when Jesus is in the wilderness being tempted by the devil.

Before you start reading, consider how God is looking at you with great love. Pray for God's grace as you enter the passage and ask Jesus to teach you to know him more clearly, love him more dearly and follow him more nearly, day by day. Read through the passage several times, letting the scene sink into your mind until you can set the Bible aside and enter the scene with your imagination. Reflect on the scene as you imagine yourself there. What do you experience? What do you do? What do you feel? What does Jesus say to you? You may like to talk out loud to Jesus.

At the end of your prayer time talk with Jesus, as with a dearly loved friend. Thank him for who he is and what he has done for you and how he has led you in *Imaginative Prayer.* Journal the outcome.

Examen
During the day or evening, reflect on when you felt moved towards God and his love, and when you felt distant from him, which resulted in you feeling sad or uncomfortable. What are you most grateful for and what are you least grateful for this day? What brought you closer to God or what drained you and led you away from God? Offer these moments to God in prayer and thankfulness that you can talk to him, and he listens. Journal the outcome. If you have children, you may like to do the *Examen* together.

Day 18

Three Forms of Love

Contemplation

Saint Ignatius of Loyola writes about three forms of love which grow progressively deeper. He names them "fidelity", "loving care" and "compassion". The first is faithful love and this type of love is a steadfast commitment of one person to another in their love. With this kind of love, nothing in the world can tempt a person from making a choice that would damage the relationship. The next love is caring love, and this is shown through those who love so deeply and care so much for another person, that they freely put aside their own desires and any selfishness to put the other person first. When a couple marries in the Church of England each person may use the vows of the Church to each other which commit in word and prayer to this caring love.

> I, (name), take you, (name)
> to be my wife/husband,
> to have and to hold
> from this day forward;
> for better, for worse,
> for richer, for poorer,
> in sickness and in health,
> to love and to cherish,
> till death us do part,
> according to God's holy law.
> In the presence of God I make this vow.[58]

Finally, compassionate love is a love that is understood by the heart. This person's true desire is not only to care for another, regardless of whether the circumstances are hard or good, but also to share everything in life with the other person. This person will share in the sufferings, poverty, humiliation, and whatever life throws at the person they love, so they share this together.

In *You Are What You Love*, the author declares that what we want or desire and what we love are connected and are saying the same thing, as "our wants and longings and desires are at the core of our identity, the wellspring from which our actions and behavior flows.[59] It is God who teaches us to love, so we need to align our desires or loves to his desires and loves, which takes time. Saint Augustine writes of God "You awaken us to delight in Your praise, You made us for Yourself, and our hearts are restless until they rest in You."[60] He says we are made to worship God and be with him, and anything that draws us away from God's presence will cause us to lose our peace, as we will be offering our worship to something other than him. We will desire and search, until we find love in Christ, which was what we were desiring all along, but did not know. Entertainment does not form us in Christ or give us love and it is not everlasting. It can give us short bursts of joy, but what we really desire is that deep fellowship of love with Christ and others and, like any deep relationship, this takes time and commitment.

Going back to these three forms of love described by Saint Ignatius, he moves us to consider them as "three kinds of love for God". Faithful love, which is a gift from God, is the kind of love whereby nothing in the world can tempt a person from making a choice that would damage their relationship with God, even if it were the only way to save their life from death. Caring love shows through one who loves Christ so deeply that the person freely puts aside their own desires and any selfishness because they only desire what Christ desires and want to be always attentive to him. Whether they are rich or poor, sick, or healthy, have a long life or a short one, they desire to follow God's call on their life. Finally, compassionate love is the love understood by the heart. This is a gift from God and leads to the person desiring poverty, so the person will be with the poor, desiring to be considered worthless by the world, because Jesus was considered worthless. They love Jesus so deeply that they want to become what he was on earth and to deepen their love with him in every way.

Reflection

Is there a habit or practice in your life which is not drawing you to love and be formed by Christ? Can you give up this habit or practice and ask Christ to help you? Do you find discipleship challenging? Talk with Jesus about this as you would with a dearly loved friend. Journal the outcome.

Scripture

Today, reflect on scripture using *Imaginative Prayer*. In *Imaginative Prayer* you read the scripture several times until you have the story in your mind, then put the passage aside and reflect on the story in your mind. Play the story back as you reflect and imagine what is going on. The scripture is John 1:35-42 when Jesus asks two of John the Baptist's disciples, "What do you want?" You might be yourself, or one of the disciples, in the story. What is happening? What is Jesus like? Does he call you? Do you follow? Where do you go? Smell the sea and sand, and even the fish, as you enter the story. Hear the wind and the waves lapping on the shore. If you go to where Jesus is staying, are you given food? What is the conversation? Reflect on what you desire and want as you imagine being there on the shore. You may want to talk to Jesus and the disciples and listen to what they say back.

Before you start reading, consider how God is looking at you with great love. Pray for God's grace as you enter the passage and ask Jesus to teach you to know him more clearly, love him more dearly and follow him more nearly, day by day. Read the passage several times, letting the scene sink into your mind until you can set the Bible aside and enter the scene with your imagination. Reflect on what is happening as you imagine yourself there. What do you experience? What do you do? What do you feel? What does Jesus say to you?

At the end of your prayer time talk with Jesus, as with a dearly loved friend. Thank him for who he is and what he has done for you, and how he has led you in *Imaginative Prayer*. Journal the outcome.

Poem

Charlotte Mew was an English poet from the Victorian era. One of her poems is called "In the Fields".

Examen

During the day or evening, reflect on when you felt moved towards

God and his love, and when you felt distant from him, which resulted in you feeling sad or uncomfortable. What are you most grateful for and what are you least grateful for this day? What brought you life and closer to God, and what drained you of life and led you away from God? Offer these moments to God in prayer and thankfulness that you can talk to him, and he listens. Journal the outcome. If you have children, you may like to do the *Examen* together.

Day 19

Consolation/Desolation

Contemplation

You have been noticing and journaling what Holy Spirit has been doing in your life. In the *Examen*, you reflected on each day and your experience with God and when you felt moved towards God and when you felt distant from him. Today you reflect more on these feelings you experienced. These feelings have been named spiritual consolation, when we are turned towards God and others, and spiritual desolation, when we are turned towards ourselves. Francis Keenan S.J. was a faithful Irish Jesuit priest who died in 2020. He identified experiences of consolation and desolation which helped others see this more clearly in their own lives. Ponder on these words he has left us to help you recognise when you are experiencing spiritual consolation and turning towards God and others, and when you are turned towards yourself and experiencing desolation.

> **Spiritual Consolation: Experiences which turn us towards God and others**
>
> Confidence in God's love for us and for the world.
>
> Awareness of the active presence of God's creative love in my life and the world.
>
> Movement of love or desire towards God.
>
> Any experience which deepens and strengthens the above.
>
> Appreciation of the value of my life and gifts as being God's gifts to me.
>
> Awareness of my own sinfulness and my need for God's healing and forgiveness.
>
> Experience of inner freedom or of being liberated in any way.

Feeling of harmony within myself, with others and with God.

Urge to be part of the struggle to spread the Kingdom, truth, and justice, whatever the cost.

Readiness to respond to the call of Christ, even at personal cost.

Sense of a person, event, or place as being a sacrament of the presence of God for me.

Any attraction to the greater good.

Experiences of Desolation: These turn us towards self

Feeling that God seems absent from my life.

Sense of God's absence from the events of my own life and from those of the world.

Diminishing confidence in God and his love, which leads to discouragement.

Inability to experience trust in or accept God's goodness.

Sense of being at odds with oneself and with God.

Any movement of love or desire which takes me away from God.

Any attraction to what is less good.

Sense that my life is empty and meaningless.

Feeling of being trapped in a circle of remorse and guilt at my own sinfulness.

Feeling of not being free, or being paralysed by fear, anxiety, and attachments.

Apparent inability to meet God in any way.

State of self-disgust or self-hatred.

Aversion to anything which has to do with the reign of God.

Reluctance or even unwillingness to serve others in the name of Christ.

Feeling of revulsion or fear at the prospect of following Christ, especially towards suffering.

As we attune to consolation and desolation within our lives, we attune to where God is leading us and what brings us life, as we live according to his desires which become our desires. Notice that Keenan mentions an "attraction to the greater good" which draws us into consolation, and an "attraction to what is less good", which leads us into desolation. As we discern what God has for our lives, there may be two good paths or opportunities, and either could be good for us, but which path or opportunity leads us into God's presence and his desire for our life and which draws us away? When I was working in gardening, I had a desire to return to be a Christian missionary, but I was not sure if it was right. I reflected on my life and where in my gardening job I experienced consolation and where I experienced desolation. I then reflected on my time within YWAM, the Christian mission organisation in which I had previously worked, and the consolation and desolation I had experienced in missions. Over time I sensed more consolation as I thought of returning to YWAM, and a sense of love and desire for God as I reflected on this vocation. This deepened when I returned to work again in missions. Both vocations appeared good, but one was leading me towards God and into consolation and so "the greater good", and one was leading me away from God and into desolation. Jesus desires for all people to know the truth about who they are and to know their need for him. Without Christ we do not bear fruit in anything we do,[61] so let us grow in being obedient to him, wherever we go and whatever we do.

Reflection
Reflect on your life and where you experience spiritual consolation, which turns you towards God and others, and where you experience spiritual desolation, which leads you to turn in on yourself and away from God and others. Offer these experiences to God, and talk to him about them, and listen to what he has to say to you. Talk with Jesus, as with a dearly loved friend. Thank him for who he is, what he has done for you and what he will do for you. Journal the outcome.

Scripture and Imaginative Prayer
Today, reflect on scripture using *Imaginative Prayer*. In *Imaginative Prayer* you read the scripture several times until you have the story in your mind, then put the passage aside and reflect on the story in your mind. Play the story back as you reflect and imagine what is going on. The scripture is Luke 5:1-11. Jesus asks Simon Peter if he can borrow his

boat to stand in and preach to the people on the shore. Then Jesus shows Simon Peter what his ministry will be by providing him with an enormous catch of fish. Reflect on this passage and what is going on. You might imagine yourself as one of the disciples, or someone in the crowd. What is happening? What is Jesus like? What is he saying? Does he speak to you?

Before you start reading, consider how God is looking at you with great love. Pray for God's grace as you enter the passage and ask Jesus to teach you to know him more clearly, love him more dearly, and follow him more nearly, day by day. Read the passage several times, letting the scene sink into your mind until you can set the Bible aside and enter the scene with your imagination. Reflect on what is happening as you imagine yourself there. What do you experience? What do you do? What do you feel? What does Jesus say to you?

At the end of your prayer time talk with Jesus, as with a dearly loved friend. Thank him for who he is and what he has done for you, and how he has led you in *Imaginative Prayer.* Journal the outcome.

Examen

Reflect on when you felt moved towards God and his love, and when you felt distant from him, which resulted in you feeling sad or uncomfortable. What brought you consolation, life, and closeness to God, and what drained you of life, and brought desolation as you turned inwards towards yourself and away from God? Offer these moments to God in prayer and thankfulness that you can talk to him, and he listens. Journal the outcome.

Day 20

Awareness and Acceptance

Contemplation

As you have been contemplating over these last weeks, you may have become more aware of Christ in your life. You may have become more aware of your gifts, your sins, the world which influences your choices, and aspects of your life which were previously hidden. Spend time today looking over and reflecting on what you have written in your journal. You may notice roots which keep you strong in Christ, or weeds which you are finding hard to uproot. Be aware of where you are, and accept that Christ deeply loves you, and he is doing a deep work within you.

As you reflect on the evening *Examen*, you may notice a pattern in consolation, as you see yourself drawn to Christ, and experience life and joy, or desolation, where you see yourself drawn away from Christ's presence. You may notice repeated moods or feelings, words, or phrases, which show you where Holy Spirit is leading you, or where you are going away from Christ. You may notice that a particular scriptural passage touched you. Maybe Jesus' dream and invitation to you, which is your personal vocation, has become more personal to you. Journal the outcome of your reflection.

Reflection

What is Christ's personal invitation to you that you see within the pages of your journal? This might be a commitment to spend more quality time with Father, Son, and Holy Spirit, or it might be accepting a work that Holy Spirit is offering you, or believing a truth revealed to you. It could be anything, and it is from Jesus specifically for you, so it will be what you desire. Write down in your journal your response to Christ's invitation to you and pray that you can commit to this invitation.

Scripture
Today, as you have been thinking about your own faith and trust in Christ, you can enter scripture with the disciples as their faith and trust in Jesus deepen. There are three scriptures, and you can choose one of them to reflect on using *Imaginative Prayer*. In *Imaginative Prayer* you read the scripture several times until you have the story in your mind, then put the scripture aside and reflect on the story in your mind. Play the story back as you reflect and imagine what is going on.

The scriptures to choose from are Luke 8:22-25 when Jesus calms the storm, Luke 9:1-10 when the twelve disciples go on a mission, and Luke 9:28-36, which is the transfiguration when Jesus meets with Moses and Elijah. Who are you? You might be yourself or one of the disciples in the story. What is happening? What is Jesus like? What is he saying? Does he speak to you? Enter the scene and imagine being there. Is there an invitation Jesus is offering you?

Before you start reading, choose which scripture you will contemplate and then consider how God is looking at you with great love. Pray for God's grace as you enter the passage and ask Jesus to teach you to know him more clearly, love him more dearly and follow him more nearly, day by day. If you get distracted, come back to this prayer of asking for God's grace and asking Jesus to teach you to know him more clearly, love him more dearly and follow him more nearly, trusting that Holy Spirit will lead you in your thoughts and within the passage. Read the passage several times, letting the scene sink into your mind until you can set the Bible aside and enter the scene with your imagination. What do you experience? What does Jesus say to you?

At the end of your prayer time talk with Jesus, as with a dearly loved friend. Thank him for who he is and what he has done for you, and how he has led you in *Imaginative Prayer*. Journal the outcome.

Poem
Today is another poem by Mary Oliver called "Praying", which reveals her sense of prayerfulness as she reflects on nature.

Examen
Reflect on when you felt moved towards God and his love, and when

you felt distant from him, which resulted in you feeling sad or uncomfortable. What brought you consolation, life and closer to God, or what drained you of life and brought desolation as you turned inwards towards yourself and away from God? Offer these moments to God in prayer and thankfulness that you can talk to him, and he listens. Journal the outcome.

Day 21

Christ's love

Contemplation

Today, use your creative imagination as you contemplate love. Christ loves you, but what is love and how aware are you of the love he has for you and all creation? God loves everything that he has made and that includes you. As you accept this love, you become a lover of all that Christ loves. Love presents itself in action and deeds, and love involves sharing with others. In the book of Acts, the apostle Paul told the Ephesian church that he remembered "the words of the Lord Jesus, how he himself said, 'It is more blessed to give than to receive.'"[62] In Christ, we give knowledge, wisdom, wealth, or another benefit that can draw another to receive love and may enable them to more freely give and love as Christ gives and loves.

Practical

If you are able, go for a walk in a garden, park, or the countryside, and appreciate God's creation. Smell a flower and receive the beautiful fragrance the flower gives back to you. Feel the texture of the leaves or petals and contemplate the grandeur of a tree. Delight in the beauty of the birds and insects. Be aware that Christ delights in you and accept that Christ deeply loves you, and he is doing a deep work within you.

Reflection

Imagine that you are standing or sitting with Christ, and around you are his angels and those saints who have gone before you. Imagine there are people there who have prayed for you and are now with Christ. Imagine yourself there with them. Pray for Jesus to give you a deep-felt appreciation of all the blessings he has given you, which fills you with thankfulness and the desire to love and serve Christ in every way. Reflect on these gifts, family members, and friends, and how Christ has created and redeemed you and continues to. Reflect on Christ's love for you, what he has done for you, and how much he has given to you. Christ gives you his very self for you to receive. You may want to end with the following Ignatian prayer, as a response of gratitude before you journal the outcome.

> Take, Lord, and receive all my liberty, my memory, my understanding, and my entire will, all that I have and possess. You gave it all to me; to you I return it. All is yours, dispose of it entirely according to your will. Give me only the love of you together with your grace, for that is enough for me.[63]

Scripture

The scripture today is John 11:1-12:11 and it is a long passage about the raising of Lazarus from death, the reaction of the authorities, and the supper at Bethany when Mary pours perfume on Jesus's feet. You may want to reflect on the whole passage or a few verses that Holy Spirit leads you to contemplate upon. Reflect on the scripture using *Imaginative Prayer*. In *Imaginative Prayer* you read the scripture several times until you have the story in your mind, then put the passage aside and reflect on the story in your mind. Play the story back as you reflect and imagine what is going on.

Before you start reading, consider how God is looking at you with great love. Pray for God's grace that as you enter the passage, he gives you a deep-felt knowledge of Jesus and what he values, so you can love him more and follow him more closely. Pray Jesus will help you to understand his mind and heart as he committed himself to go through with his Father's desire for him, no matter what. Read the passage several times, letting the scene sink into your mind until you can set the Bible aside and enter the scene with your imagination. Reflect on what is happening as you imagine yourself there. Who are you? Are you one in the crowd, a disciple, or are you Mary or Martha, or yourself? What do you feel? What does Jesus say?

At the end of your prayer time talk with Jesus, as with a dearly loved friend. Thank him for who he is and what he has done for you, and how he has led you in *Imaginative Prayer*. Journal the outcome.

Poem
The poem today is by the 20th century American poet, Robert Frost, and it is called "A Prayer in Spring".

Examen
Reflect on when you felt moved towards God and his love, and when you felt distant from him, which resulted in you feeling sad or uncomfortable. What are you most grateful for and what are you least grateful for this day? What brought you life and closer to God, and what drained you of life and led you away from God? Offer these moments to God in prayer and thankfulness that you can talk to him, and he listens. If you have children, you may like to do the *Examen* together, or you may like to do the *Examen* with another individual. Journal the outcome.

Day 22

Way to Jerusalem

Contemplation

Over these next days we contemplate the journey to the cross, and the crucifixion of Jesus. As we desire to share in Christ's crucifixion, we may feel dry and even desolate in our prayer time, and far from God. Stay with your feelings, and notice what is going on within you, as Christ will be deepening your relationship with him. As you pray with Christ, pray that you feel sorrow as he felt sorrow, anguish as he felt anguish, compassion as he felt compassion, and deep grief and suffering as he felt deep grief and suffering. This prayer is more passive than active as you rest, and pray to share with Christ what he experienced, so you can love him more deeply. Over these days, rest in your feelings, and see them as a gift uniting you with Christ and his suffering. The contemplations, reflections, and scriptures should lead you outwards to focus on Christ, rather than on yourself. You may want to meditate on scripture, or just be with Jesus in silence, and reflect on him and the cross. You may want to sit with Jesus, thinking about him, or you could use the practice of Centering Prayer from Day One (see below).

The Practice of Centering Prayer[64]

1. Choose a sacred word such as Abba, Father, Jesus, Spirit, love, peace etc. You can ask Jesus for a word that is specific to you at this time.
2. Sit in a comfortable, quiet place. Close your eyes. Breathe in and out, noticing your breath. Introduce the word into your mind and reflect on the word as you breathe in and as you breathe out. You are inviting the presence of God into your life and opening yourself to him.
3. If distractions occur, gently unite yourself with the word

and so with God's presence, who longs to be with you.

4. At the end of the prayer time keep silent, with your eyes closed, for a few minutes.

5. You have spent precious time in God's presence. Stand up and stretch and carry on with your life.

Reflection

Walk outside, or sit in a comfortable position, and imagine you are walking or sitting with Jesus and his angels and saints who have gone before you. Think of the people who have prayed for you and are now with Jesus. Imagine yourself there with them. Pray for Jesus to give you a deep-felt appreciation of all the blessings he has given you, which fills you with thankfulness and desire to love and serve Christ in every way. Reflect on how God dwells in his creatures, and how he reveals himself in the gifts he gives. He gives plants their existence and life, as they need light, carbon dioxide, and water, all provided for them by him and us. He gives life to animals, birds, butterflies, beetles, and all other insects. Slow down and watch or imagine these creatures, and the gifts God has given them. God dwells in us and gives us life, intelligence, and freedom, and we are his temple, made in his image and likeness. You may want to end with the following Ignatian prayer, as a response of gratitude before you journal the outcome.

> Take, Lord, and receive all my liberty, my memory, my understanding, and my entire will, all that I have and possess. You gave it all to me; to you I return it. All is yours, dispose of it entirely according to your will. Give me only the love of you together with your grace, for that is enough for me.[65]

Scripture

The scripture for *Imaginative Prayer* today is from John 12:12-19, when Jesus rides into Jerusalem on a donkey. In *Imaginative Prayer* you read the scripture several times until you have the story in your mind, then put the passage aside and reflect on the story in your mind. Play the story back as you reflect and imagine what is going on. Are you in the crowd shouting 'Hosanna' or are you looking at what is happening? Do you, like the disciples, not understand what is going on? What do you feel? Does Jesus speak to you or say anything? What is the look on his face?

Before you start reading, consider how God is looking at you with great love. Pray for God's grace as you enter the passage and ask Jesus that you might experience his sorrow and compassion, as he is going to suffer for our sin. Read the passage several times, letting the scene sink into your mind until you can set the Bible aside and enter the scene with your imagination. Reflect on what is happening as you imagine yourself there. What do you experience? What do you do? What do you feel? What does Jesus say to you?

At the end of your prayer time talk with Jesus, as with a dearly loved friend. Thank him for who he is and what he has done for you, and how he has led you in *Imaginative Prayer*. Journal the outcome.

Poem

Consider, "The Poet thinks about the Donkey" by Mary Oliver, as you reflect on the Passion.

Examen

Reflect on when you felt moved towards God and his love, and when you felt distant from him, which resulted in you feeling sad or uncomfortable. What are you most grateful for and what are you least grateful for this day? What brought you life and closer to God, and what drained you of life and led you away from God? Offer these moments to God in prayer and thankfulness that you can talk to him, and he listens. If you have children, you may like to do the *Examen* together, or you may like to do the *Examen* with another individual. Journal the outcome.

Day 23

Judas Betrays Jesus

Contemplation

Today, we wait, watch, and accompany Jesus on his last day of freedom before he is arrested and crucified. Although Jesus has spoken several times to his disciples about what will happen, they still do not understand. The crowds of people attending the Passover festival are unaware of the true Lamb of God who is about to be slaughtered. There may be people who wonder if he will succeed in what he came for or believe he will fail. There may be those who shouted "Hosanna" and laid palm branches at his feet who wonder what he will do next or wonder what he has come for. Are you one of them? If you can, lay aside what you know about Jesus so you can accompany him and enter his story.

Jesus had a choice in everything he did, and he had a choice to enter Jerusalem. As Jesus listened to his Father, did his Father reveal everything to him at once as to how and when his life would end, or was it a gradual reveal? There were many who doubted Jesus's true identity and as we accompany him, maybe we doubt who he is. We might doubt words he has spoken to us. We accompany Jesus, and we too have a choice to spend time with him. Can we follow him, going to lonely places to pray, and be with him, or are we distracted by the world and all it has to offer? Jesus loved his family and friends, but he never placed them before his Father.

This is an invitation for you to accompany Jesus and contemplate him. Pray for his gift of sorrow and compassion as you accompany him in his sufferings for sin. Be aware that you may feel desolate and if you are, ask Holy Spirit what is going on that you feel this way. As Christ bore fruit through suffering, so we bear fruit through desolation.

You may want to end with the following Ignatian prayer, as a response of gratitude before you journal the outcome.

Take, Lord, and receive all my liberty, my memory, my understanding, and my entire will, all that I have and possess. You gave it all to me; to you I return it. All is yours, dispose of it entirely according to your will. Give me only the love of you together with your grace, for that is enough for me.[66]

Scripture

The scripture for *Imaginative Prayer* today is Matthew 26:14-30. Judas betrays Jesus, the Passover is prepared and eaten, and the Eucharist is initiated. You may want to enter the whole passage, or you may feel led to reflect on a few verses or part of the story. In *Imaginative Prayer* you read the scripture several times until you have the story in your mind, then put the passage aside and reflect on the story in your mind. Decide whether you will reflect on a portion of the scripture or the whole passage before prayer. Play the story back as you reflect and imagine what is going on. Who are you? What do you feel? Do you speak to Judas? Does Jesus speak to you or say anything? What is the look on his face? Does he give you the bread and wine?

Before you start reading, consider how God is looking at you with great love. Pray for God's grace as you enter the passage, and ask Jesus that you might experience his sorrow and compassion as he is going to suffer for our sin. Read the passage several times, letting the scene sink into your mind until you can set the Bible aside and enter the scene with your imagination. Reflect on what is happening as you imagine yourself there. What do you experience? What do you do? What do you feel? What does Jesus say to you?

At the end of your prayer time talk with Jesus, as with a dearly loved friend. Thank him for who he is and what he has done for you and how he has led you in *Imaginative Prayer*. You may like to end with the following prayer. Journal the outcome.

The Anima Christi

Jesus, fashion me wholly in your image.
By your Body and blood
Sustain me in your way.
By your passion and death
Strengthen my faltering will.

May I seek shelter nowhere
But in the shadow of your Cross.
In loneliness and doubt
Let your presence be enough for me.
Keep me safe from evil,
And never let me forsake your love.
Shed your light and love
On all my partings and goodbyes,
And help me to let go.
Keep my gaze ever fixed on you
Until at last you call me Home
To praise you with your saints forever.
Amen. (Version by Michael McCabe)

Examen
Reflect on when you felt moved towards God and his love, and when you felt distant from him, which resulted in you feeling sad or uncomfortable. For what are you most grateful and for what are you least grateful this day? What brought you life and closer to God, and what drained you of life and led you away from God? Offer these moments to God in prayer and thankfulness that you can talk to him, and he listens. If you have children, you may like to do the *Examen* together, or you may like to do the *Examen* with another individual. Journal the outcome.

Day 24

Jesus and the Cross

Contemplation

Adam and Eve were created in the image of God, and God dwelt with them in the Temple Garden of Eden. It was effectively the first temple because it was the place where God dwelt with his people. They knew God, and they had everything they needed. Satan was lying when he slithered into their lives and told them they would be like God if they ate from the tree that God told them not to eat from. They <u>were</u> like God. When Adam and Eve ate the apple, they were not just eating a piece of fruit, but they were turning away from the truth of what God had told them and tucking into death. God told them they would die, and they died spiritually, as evil, sin and death entered humanity. They could no longer live in the Temple Garden, where there was the opportunity to eat from the tree of life and live eternally in this fallen state. That would be too awful, so God had to turn them out of the garden.[67] But he never gave up on people.

God always intended to dwell with his people in a place where there would be no evil, sin, or death. It was always God's plan that Jesus would be King, fully human, and fully God, and reign with his people. Since sin and death came into the world through Adam's and Eve's rebellion in the Temple Garden, something had to happen to bring restoration to humankind. Someone needed to defeat Satan, and in doing that defeat sin and death, and restore humanity to their rightful relationship with God, and to care for creation as God intended.

Jesus was fully God as his mother, Mary, became pregnant by the Holy Spirit, not by another man. He was also fully human, as he was born of Mary. Jesus was and is God, and he entered fully into humanity. As Adam and Eve were made in God's image, God's image bearers, Jesus too was born from a woman and was God's image

98

bearer, but he was also "the exact imprint of his [Father's] nature".[68] Jesus understood everything about being human, and yet he did not sin. He listened to his Father, even being obedient unto death on the cross. As sin and death had entered the world through Adam because he rebelled, Jesus, the second Adam, embraced "the sin and suffering of the whole world, taking it into himself on the cross and destroying its power over us in his resurrection".[69] Jesus showed humanity what it was to be fully human, so we could once again live as God intended, by the Holy Spirit. He showed humanity how to live as image bearers, to contemplate the beauty of the Father and creation and to participate in his good purposes.

The only way for humanity to unite once again in eternal life and love in Father, Son, and Holy Spirit, was for God to enter our sin and death, defeat this evil, and personally bring us back into this loving relationship. Jesus Christ, who was and is fully God, became fully human. Being born into this world through the virgin Mary, he lived an ordinary life with all the challenges of the human condition, and he grew to be a wise man, formed through scripture, and prayer to his Father. Jesus was tempted like every other man, and yet he did not sin, but lived in faithful obedience to his Father all his life. He healed people, preached the good news of the kingdom of God, and offered forgiveness, and the Roman and Jewish forces killed him. The Temple leaders were still in rebellion and could not accept a God who would not do life their way. In our rebellion, we are greedy, lustful, and violent, as we focus on our own choices, trying to work out our own salvation to find happiness.

When Passover arrived, the festival to celebrate Israel's release from slavery to freedom, Jesus rode into Jerusalem, and in doing so started a revolution that would lead to his crucifixion. The Roman and Jewish forces arrested and crucified him because he was the fulfilment of the suffering servant image in Isaiah, and he understood his vocation as Messiah. He started a revolution by riding into Jerusalem at Passover because he knew he was the true Passover lamb. As the lambs were being slaughtered for the Passover feast, and the Jewish people remembered how Israel had crossed the Red Sea from slavery to freedom, Jesus was being crucified. Jesus' death brought life. because death could not defeat him. He crushed the head of the serpent, as Yahweh had said he would in Genesis 3. He was wounded, but he redeemed the world from death and his death brought life to all. He went to the cross in his humanity and lovingly took the sin of man's evil upon himself. He trusted his Father would raise him from death to life, and through this the power that death had over humanity was broken.

Jesus, God's true image bearer, undid what Adam had done, taking away sin and death, and offering a new way to be human. He brought in a new covenant and initiated a ritual of baptism to connect new believers to his death and resurrection. He introduced a new meal to share together as the disciples broke bread and drank wine in remembrance of his body and blood in the crucifixion. The only way for humanity to unite once again in eternal life and love in the Father, Son, and Holy Spirit, was for God to enter our sin and death, defeat this evil, and personally bring us back into this loving relationship.

This is an invitation for you to accompany Jesus and contemplate his sacrifice. Pray for his gift of sorrow and compassion as you accompany him in his sufferings for sin. Be aware that you may feel desolate and if you are, ask Holy Spirit what is going on that you feel this way. As Christ bore fruit through suffering, so we bear fruit through desolation. What does the cross mean to you? Talk to Jesus about this as you would with a dearly loved friend.

Reflection

As you reflect on what Jesus has done for you and how much he loves you, you may like to break bread and drink wine with others in remembrance of his body and blood in the crucifixion. We are united in his death and so united in his life. You may like to pray the following response of gratitude.

> Take, Lord, and receive all my liberty, my memory, my understanding, and my entire will, all that I have and possess. You gave it all to me; to you I return it. All is yours, dispose of it entirely according to your will. Give me only the love of you together with your grace, for that is enough for me.[70]

Scripture

The scripture for *Imaginative Prayer* today could be one of many, from the journey to the garden of Gethsemane and Jesus' agony as he asks his disciples to keep watch. There is the betrayal by Judas which leads to Jesus's arrest, the unjust trials and Jesus spending the night in a cell. There may be a specific scripture and story that Holy Spirit brings to your mind to focus on and contemplate, and if this is the case, then go with that. Otherwise, focus on Matthew 27:27-38, Mark 15:16-27, Luke 23:26-34 or John 19:17-22, which is when Jesus is taken to be crucified. Choose the scripture you feel led to before you start your time of prayer.

You may want to enter the whole passage, or you may feel led to reflect on a few verses or part of the story. In *Imaginative Prayer* you read the scripture several times until you have the story in your mind, then put the passage aside and reflect on the story in your mind. Play the story back as you reflect and imagine what is going on. Who are you? What do you feel? Does Jesus speak to you or say anything? What is the look on his face?

Before you start reading, consider how God is looking at you with great love. Pray for God's grace as you enter the passage and ask Jesus that you might experience his sorrow and compassion as he is going to suffer for our sin. Read the passage several times, letting the scene sink into your mind until you can set the Bible aside and enter the scene with your imagination. Reflect on what is happening as you imagine yourself there. What do you experience? What do you do? What do you feel? What does Jesus say to you?

At the end of your prayer time talk with Jesus, as with a dearly loved friend. Thank him for who he is and what he has done for you and how he has led you in *Imaginative Prayer*. You may like to end with the following prayer. Journal the outcome.

The Anima Christi
Jesus, fashion me wholly in your image.
By your Body and blood
Sustain me in your way.
By your passion and death
Strengthen my faltering will.
May I seek shelter nowhere
But in the shadow of your Cross.
In loneliness and doubt
Let your presence be enough for me.

Keep me safe from evil,
And never let me forsake your love.
Shed your light and love
On all my partings and goodbyes,
And help me to let go.
Keep my gaze ever fixed on you
Until at last you call me Home
To praise you with your saints forever.
Amen. (Version by Michael McCabe)

Examen

Reflect on when you felt moved towards God and his love, and when you felt distant from him, which resulted in you feeling sad or uncomfortable. For what are you most grateful and for what are you least grateful this day? What brought you life and closer to God or what drained you of life and led you away from God? Offer these moments to God in prayer and thankfulness that you can talk to him, and he listens. If you have children, you may like to do the *Examen* together, or you may like to do the *Examen* with another individual. Journal the outcome.

Day 25

Crucifixion

Contemplation

As we contemplate the crucifixion of Christ, and the sorrow and distress of his family, friends, and disciples, we ask Jesus to gift us with his sorrow and compassion, so we experience a little of what he went through, and what those he loved went through. We ask that we might understand more deeply why he died and suffered for us in this way, which will move us to love him more. The words today are from an article by the Canadian Catholic priest, Father Ronald Rolheiser.

When Jesus sweated blood in the Garden of Gethsemane and asked his Father to let the cup of suffering pass him by, he wasn't, for the most part, cringing before the prospect of brute physical suffering. He was cringing before the prospect of a very particular kind of suffering that is generally more feared than physical pain. When he asked God if it was really necessary to die in this way he was referring to more than death through capital punishment.

Crucifixion was devised and designed by the Romans with more than one thing in mind. It was designed as capital punishment, to put a criminal to death, but it aimed to do a couple of other things as well.

It was designed to inflict optimal physical pain. Thus the procedure was dragged out over a good number of hours and the amount of pain inflicted at any given moment was carefully calculated so as not to cause unconsciousness and thus ease the pain of the one being crucified. Indeed they sometimes even gave wine mixed with morphine to the person being crucified, not to ease his suffering, but to keep him from passing out from pain so as to have to endure it longer.

But crucifixion was designed with still another even more callous intent. It was designed to humiliate the person. Among other things, the person was stripped naked before being hung on a cross so that his genitals would be publicly exposed. As well, at the moment of death his bowels would loosen. Crucifixion clearly had humiliation in mind.

We have tended to downplay this aspect, both in our preaching and in our art. We have, as Jurgens Moltmann put it, surrounded the cross with roses, with aesthetic and antiseptic wrapping towels. But that was not the case for Jesus. His nakedness was exposed, his body publicly humiliated. That, among other reasons, is why the crucifixion was such a devastating blow to his disciples and why many of them abandoned Jesus and scattered after the crucifixion. They simply couldn't connect this kind of humiliation with glory, divinity, and triumph.

Interestingly there is a striking parallel between what crucifixion did to the human body and what nature itself often does to the human body through old age, cancer, dementia, AIDS, and diseases such as Parkinson's, Lou Gehrig's, Huntington's, and other such sicknesses that humiliate the body before killing it. They expose publicly what is most vulnerable inside of our humanity. They shame the body.

Why? What is the connection between this type of pain and the glory of Easter Sunday? Why is it, as the gospels say, "necessary to first suffer in this manner so as to enter into glory?"

Because, paradoxically, a certain depth of soul can only be attained through a certain depth of humiliation. How and why is this so? It isn't easy to articulate rationally but we can understand this through experience:

Ask yourself this question with courage and honesty: What experiences in my life have made me deep? In virtually every case, I will venture to say, experiences that have deepened you will be incidences that you feel some shame in acknowledging, a powerlessness from which you were unable to protect yourself, an abuse from which you could not defend yourself, an inadequacy of body or mind that has left you vulnerable, a humiliating incident that once happened to you, or some mistake you made which publicly exposed your lack of strength in some area. All of us, like Jesus, have also been, in one way or another, hung up publicly and humiliated. And we have depth of soul to just that extent.

But depth of soul comes in very different modes. Humiliation makes us deep, but we can be deep in character, understanding, graciousness, and forgiveness or we can be deep in anger, bitterness, revenge-seeking, and murder. Jesus' crucifixion stretched his heart and made it huge in empathy, graciousness, and forgiveness. But it doesn't always work that way. Many of our worst mass-murderers have also experienced deep humiliation and it too has stretched their hearts, except in their case it has made them deep in bitterness, callousness, and murder.

Several summers ago, I was at a conference at the University of Notre Dame where the Holy Cross community had gathered to prepare itself for the Beatification of its founder. Reflecting upon the spirituality of their founder, one Holy Cross member offered this challenge to his community: If you live inside of any family for any length of the time, at some point that family will wound you and wound you deeply. But, and this is the point, how you handle that wound, with either bitterness or forgiveness, will color the rest of your life!

In the crucifixion, Jesus was humiliated, shamed, brutalized. That pain stretched his heart to a great depth. But that new space did not fill in with bitterness and anger. It filled in instead with a depth of empathy and forgiveness that we have yet to fully understand.[71]

105

Scripture

The scripture for *Imaginative Prayer* today is from the day of the crucifixion and death of Christ. There are four passages to choose from in the gospels: Matthew 27:39-56, Mark 15:29-41, Luke 23:35-49 or John 19:23-37. Again, choose the passage you feel most led to contemplate on this day and decide on the passage before you enter prayer. You may want to reflect on the whole passage, or you may feel led to reflect on a few verses, or part of the story. In imaginative prayer you read the scripture several times until you have the story in your mind, then put the scripture aside and reflect on the story in your mind. Decide whether you will reflect on a portion of the scripture or the whole passage before prayer. Play the story back as you reflect and imagine what is going on. Who are you? What do you feel? Does Jesus speak to you or say anything? What is the look on his face? Do you talk to Mary or any of the other women? Are you there at the cross or are you looking from a distance?

Before you start reading, consider how God is looking at you with great love. Pray for God's grace as you enter the passage and ask Jesus that you might experience his sorrow and compassion as he is going to suffer for our sin. Read the passage several times, letting the scene sink into your mind until you can set the Bible aside and enter the scene with your imagination. Reflect on what is happening as you imagine yourself there. What do you experience? What do you do? What do you feel? What does Jesus say to you?

At the end of your prayer time talk with Jesus, as with a dearly loved friend. Thank him for who he is and what he has done for you and how he has led you in *Imaginative Prayer*. Journal the outcome.

Poem

The poem today is "Stabat Mater" and it is ascribed to Jacopone da Todi. It is a Christian hymn to Mary, thought to be written in the 13th century. Originally written in Latin, there is a translation by Edward Caswell, a priest and hymn writer in the 19th century. As you reflect on this poem, identify with Mary as she watched her son die.

Examen

Reflect on when you felt moved towards God and his love, and when you felt distant from him, which resulted in you feeling sad or uncomfortable. What are you most grateful for and what are you least grateful for this day? What brought you life and closer to God, and what drained you of life and led you away from God? Offer these moments to God in prayer and thankfulness that you can talk to him, and he listens. If you have children, you may like to do the *Examen* together, or you may like to do the *Examen* with another individual. Journal the outcome.

Day 26

The Burial

Contemplation

Jesus was taken down from the cross, bound in linen with myrrh and aloes, and laid in a tomb. The gospels of Matthew, Mark, and Luke, state that Joseph, a rich man from Arimathea, who was one of Jesus' disciples, asked for Jesus' body and laid it in his own tomb. The Gospel of John says that Nicodemus, the pharisee who came to Jesus in the night to talk with him, went to Pilate to ask for Jesus' body for burial. Maybe they both went. There were women who mourned for Jesus after he was taken down from the cross. Those women, who were dear to Jesus, included his mother. They were in pain and deeply sorrowful because of what had happened. They wanted to stay with Jesus and be with him at his burial. Jesus had asked his disciple, John, to take his mother in to live with him after his death. John had accepted Jesus' request and taken Mary into his home.

There were others affected by the death of Jesus. There was Peter, who had fulfilled Jesus' prophetic words that he would deny him. There were other disciples, who had said they would follow Jesus to the end but had fled after Jesus' arrest. Lazarus had died and had been raised to life, but did he believe that Jesus would do the same? There were all those people who had listened to Jesus' teachings, and the five thousand and four thousand who had shared bread and fish with him. Did all those people who had been healed or delivered of evil spirits have mourn Jesus' death?

One wonders what effect Jesus' death had on the city of Jerusalem at a time when the Passover festival was happening. The Passover festival was a time of celebration, as the Jews remembered how God had brought them out of slavery, miraculously across the Red Sea, and into freedom and the promised land. And yet, the Messiah they thought would bring them freedom from the Romans had died a criminal's death on a cross. Did they celebrate or mourn at this time? What was the atmosphere in Jerusalem?

Reflection

Spend time today reflecting on the burial of Jesus, and the feelings and experiences of those close to him. You might want to walk as you reflect. You might want to sit on a rock or a log, as though you are sitting at the tomb with the women. Do you feel sorrow as Jesus is taken down from the cross and Mary goes with John to his home? Where are you? At the end of your prayer time talk with Jesus, as with a dearly loved friend. Thank him for who he is and what he has done for you. Journal the outcome.

Scripture

The scripture for *Imaginative Prayer* today is the burial of Jesus. There are four passages to choose from in the gospels: Matthew 27:57-61, Mark 15:42-47, Luke 23:50-56 or John 19:38-42. Again, choose the passage you feel most led to contemplate on this day, and decide on the passage before you enter prayer. You may want to enter the whole passage, or you may feel led to reflect on a few verses or part of the story. In *Imaginative Prayer* you read the scripture several times until you have the story in your mind, then put the scripture aside and reflect on the story in your mind. Decide whether you will reflect on a portion of the scripture or the whole passage before prayer. Play the story back as you reflect and imagine what is going on. Who are you? Are you with someone or are you by yourself? What do you feel? Does anyone speak to you, or do you say anything? Do you talk to Mary or any of the other women, or the disciples? Are you at the burial or looking on from a distance?

Before you start reading, consider how God is looking at you with great love. Pray for God's grace as you enter the passage and ask Jesus that you might experience his sorrow and compassion as he suffers for our sin. Read the passage several times, letting the scene sink into your mind until you can set the Bible aside and enter the scene with your imagination. Reflect on what is happening as you imagine yourself there. What do you experience? What do you do? What do you feel?

At the end of your prayer time talk with Jesus, as with a dearly loved friend. Thank him for who he is and what he has done for you, and how he has led you in *Imaginative Prayer*. Journal the outcome.

Examen

Reflect on when you felt moved towards God and his love, and when you felt distant from him, which resulted in you feeling sad or uncomfortable. What are you most grateful for and what are you least grateful for this day? What brought you life and closer to God, and what drained you of life and led you away from God? Offer these moments to God in prayer and thankfulness that you can talk to him, and he listens. If you have children, you may like to do the *Examen* together, or you may like to do the *Examen* with another individual. Journal the outcome.

Day 27

Sunday Morning

Contemplation

Come then, my love, my lovely one, come.

For see, winter is past, the rains are over and gone.

The flowers appear on the earth.

The season of glad songs has come.[72]

Today as you come to Christ in prayer, ask and pray that the risen Lord's joy and gladness might come upon you and surprise you. If you are feeling desolate, as the women at the tomb were feeling desolate after Jesus's death, be kind to yourself, and treat yourself gently, as the risen Christ is kind, and he is a comforter. Spend time resting quietly, being with Christ and sensing his presence. This is praying in the deepest sense, as you desire to be with the one you love, with no need to say or do anything. Activity can be an obstacle to intimacy as we seek to do something. We do not need to communicate in words, but be in communion with the one we love, by being in his presence and love. As two persons who deeply care and love one another are present in silence to one another, so be present as much as you can to Jesus.

We might not want to enter silence, and we might be tempted into activity. This is because we are afraid of intimacy and real communion, so be aware of this, and be kind to yourself in this. We are often afraid of silence when we spend time with others, and we fill the silence with activity and words. Jesus longs to gently invite us to rest with him and contemplate him. Let him take you where he wants to take you, as you abide in an attitude of openness and responsiveness to him. At the end of your prayer time talk with Jesus, as with a dearly loved friend. Thank him for who he is, and how he has led you in prayer. Journal the outcome.

Reflection

Spend time throughout the day resting in Christ and sensing his presence in the quiet. As two persons, who deeply care for and love one another, are present in silence to one another, so be present as much as you can to Jesus. Sit with him, take a walk with him in the garden, have a coffee or tea with him… think of him as you go to sleep. Allow Holy Spirit to share with you the joy of Christ, which opens your heart to him. This joy is a gift from Christ, so do not try or expect to be joyful, but be silent, patient, and honest with the gift that Jesus gives you.

Scripture

The scripture for *Imaginative Prayer* today is John 20:11-18, which is set at the tomb. In *Imaginative Prayer* you read the scripture several times until you have the story in your mind, then put the scripture aside and reflect on the story in your mind. Play the story back as you reflect and imagine what is going on. The women at the tomb were overwhelmingly desolate and were not expecting to be consoled or to receive any joy, and yet that is what they received. Are you one of the women? Are you yourself, watching the scene unfold? What do you feel? Does anyone speak to you, or do you say anything? Are you at the tomb or looking on from a distance?

Before you start reading, consider how God is looking at you with great love. Pray for God's grace as you enter the passage and pray that the risen Lord's own joy and gladness might come upon you and surprise you. Read the passage several times, letting the scene sink into your mind until you can set the Bible aside and enter the scene with your imagination. Reflect on what is happening as you imagine yourself there. What do you experience? What do you do? What do you feel?

At the end of your prayer time talk with Jesus, as with a dearly loved friend. Thank him for who he is and what he has done for you, and how he has led you in *Imaginative Prayer*. Journal the outcome.

Poem

Simone Weil was a French philosopher and political activist who lived in the earlier part of the 20th century. She died when she was only 34 years old. She wrote a poem called "The Gate".

Examen

Reflect on when you felt moved towards God and his love, and when you felt distant from him, which resulted in you feeling sad or uncomfortable. What are you most grateful for and what are you least grateful for this day? What brought you life and closer to God, and what drained you of life and led you away from God? Offer these moments to God in prayer and thankfulness that you can talk to him, and he listens. If you have children, you may like to do the *Examen* together, or you may like to do the *Examen* with another individual. Journal the outcome.

Day 28

Revelation

Contemplation

Julian of Norwich was a Christian mystic who lived in the 14th/15th century. As a child, she lived through the "Black Death", which spread across the country. Thousands of people died. As a 30-year-old adult she saw visions from God, when she was ill and close to death. When she recovered, she dedicated her life to God by becoming an anchoress to a church in Norwich. She lived as a recluse in a room adjoining the church for the rest of her life. She devoted her life to prayer, and served as a spiritual counsellor from her window that overlooked the street. It was a period in history called the Middle Ages. Visions from God were not embraced by the church, and God's love was not taught in the church. The Bible was not available in English, and people went to church out of fear of going to hell, rather than out of love and relationship with Christ. Julian witnessed a God of love and acceptance. This short excerpt is from her writings, kept secret in her lifetime, and lost for centuries, until they materialised in the 20th century and were published.

> And he showed me more, a little thing, the size of a hazelnut, on the palm of my hand, round like a ball. I looked at it thoughtfully and wondered, 'What is this?' And the answer came, 'It is all that is made.' I marvelled that it continued to exist and did not suddenly disintegrate; it was so small. And again my mind supplied the answer, 'It exists, both now and for ever, because God loves it.' In short, everything owes its existence to the love of God.
>
> In this 'little thing' I saw three truths. The first is that God made it; the second is that God loves it; and the third is that God sustains it. But what he is who is in truth

Maker, Keeper, and Lover I cannot tell, for until I am essentially united with him I can never have full rest or real happiness; in other words, until I am so joined to him that there is absolutely nothing between my God and me.[73]

Reflection
Reflect on this writing by Julian of Norwich. Maybe find a hazelnut, or another symbol of creation, as you reflect and sit, or walk, in creation. Allow Holy Spirit to speak to you about what Julian of Norwich is saying. Is there something that God has made that speaks to you, in the same way that this small thing spoke to Julian of Norwich? Journal the outcome.

Scripture
The scripture for *Imaginative Prayer* today is Luke 24:13-35. Two men walk to a village called Emmaus, and Jesus walks with them. He interprets the scriptures to them concerning himself, and he breaks bread with them as they share a meal together. What an amazing experience that must have been as Jesus taught them the Bible, and slowly their eyes were opened to understand the scriptures. Then a sudden surprise as Jesus broke bread, and they realised the One spoken of in the word, was the person walking, chatting, and sitting having a meal with them. In *Imaginative Prayer* you read the scripture several times until you have the story in your mind, then put the scripture aside and reflect on the story in your mind. Play the story back as you reflect and imagine what is going on. These men were talking about Jesus and what had happened, and suddenly the man himself joins in with the conversation. Are you with the men listening? Are you watching on? Do you go to the house for a meal too? How does the scene unfold? What do you feel? Does anyone speak to you? Do you say anything? You might want to be on the move, walking, as you pray this scripture.

Before you start reading, consider how God is looking at you with great love. Pray for God's grace as you enter the passage and pray that the risen Lord's own joy and gladness might come upon you and surprise you. Read the passage several times, letting the scene sink into your mind, until you can set the Bible aside and enter the scene with your imagination. Reflect on what is happening as you imagine yourself there. What do you experience? What do you do? What do you feel? What do you say?

At the end of your prayer time talk with Jesus, as with a dearly loved friend. Thank him for who he is, and what he has done for you, and how he has led you in *Imaginative Prayer*. Journal the outcome.

Poem

The Englishman, Philip Larkin, was a 20th century novelist, and poet. His poem today is called "The Trees".

Examen

Reflect on when you felt moved towards God and his love, and when you felt distant from him, which resulted in you feeling sad or uncomfortable. What are you most grateful for and what are you least grateful for this day? What brought you life and closer to God, and what drained you of life and led you away from God? Offer these moments to God in prayer and thankfulness that you can talk to him, and he listens. If you have children, you may like to do the *Examen* together, or you may like to do the *Examen* with another individual. Journal the outcome.

Day 29

Restoration

Contemplation

When Jesus died, he defeated the power of death and Satan because death could not defeat him. He crushed the head of the serpent, as Yahweh said he would in Genesis 3. He was wounded, but he redeemed the world from death. The eternal life, lost through rebellion in the Temple Garden of Eden, was restored through Jesus' resurrection to life. And he gave life to all who believed in him with the gift of the Holy Spirit, who is God, known as the third person of the Trinity.

Jesus was fully God, and yet entered fully into humanity. As Adam and Eve were made in God's image, God's image bearers, Jesus too was God's image bearer, and understood everything about being a human being, and yet he did not sin. He lived dependent on his Father, and Holy Spirit within him, even unto death on the cross. As sin and death had entered into the world through Adam, because he rebelled, Jesus, the second Adam, embraced "the sin and suffering of the whole world, taking it into himself on the cross and destroying its power over us in his resurrection".[74] Jesus was and is the true image bearer, and he shows humanity what it is to be truly human, living by the Holy Spirit. This broken relationship between God, and humanity when they rebelled and believed the lie of the serpent, has been restored through Jesus's death and resurrection.

According to the theologian, Julie Canlis, Calvin saw the humanity of Jesus and his life, death, and resurrection as something necessary, so we would be able to draw our life from his. It was not just to conquer sin and evil that Jesus became human but, like a fountain, his life, sanctification, and transfiguration are poured out into our lives, as he sits at the right hand of his Father. This was not always Calvin's view. Initially, he did not believe that Christ's life mattered or redeemed us. He believed that sin was a problem, which was atoned for in a legal way, by Jesus receiving God's legal judgement on the cross for us. He later came to believe that Christ's incarnation did matter, because through Jesus being fully human and fully God, he remade our humanity. He took part in every aspect of human life, without distortion or alienation to his Father, and through his life brought humanity in all its brokenness into a relationship with the Father, remade through him. Calvin understood salvation as humanity exchanging their mortal poverty and weakness, for Christ's riches and immortality. As Jesus was the Son of God and lived in obedience to the Father, we now join in relationship with the Father through Jesus Christ, and we are children of God the Father. Calvin came to realise that Christ did not just die for us and take our place in death, but we received Christ's life in all its fullness through his life, death, and resurrection. Jesus was perfectly faithful to the Father and through him, we are justified and brought into union with the Father, through the Son, by the Spirit.

Consider this view of Christ's overflowing life, given to you like a fountain, as you next take the Eucharist. His body and blood in the bread and the wine feed life to your body, soul, and spirit. You do not just reflect on his crucifixion and body given for you but receive his life that feeds and sustains. Christ did not have to come to earth to save and sanctify us, but he chose to out of love. He did not receive God's punishment for our sin on the cross, which is what some people believe, as if it was God's legal judgement for him to die on the cross. He freely chose to submit to the authorities of the world, who killed him, but this did not bring death to the world, but union with his Father and life. He showed us how to be human, and in eating his body and blood, we too choose to be sanctified and made more fully human.

Jesus, in his humanity, lived dependent upon his Father and all his Father had for him to do. He lived by the Spirit within him, in the same way that we can all live by Holy Spirit. His character was formed in the same way that our character can be formed as Holy Spirit sanctifies us. All that Jesus did, in terms of miracles and healing, he did in the power of the Spirit, and we too have this gift. Jesus showed us how to live a fully human life with Holy Spirit, so we can imitate him. He showed us what the purposes of God are for this world, and he invites us to live accordingly. Instead, we try to form ourselves in the image we want, which is our sinful failing, and we seek respect by others for who we are and what we do, but Jesus did not. Jesus sought only to glorify his Father and by God's grace, we can become more Christ-like and so more human. He not only came to defeat death and sin and draw us into union with himself, but he came to show us what it is to be a true human being, made in the image of God, and to live as God intended.

Jesus did not come to condemn or to blame, and never did condemn or blame those who had wronged him. We have no record of him returning to talk to the high priest Caiaphas, who had been involved in his arrest, for example. When Jesus returned, he came to console those who loved him and to confirm the call on their lives. The grief of Mary at the tomb turned to joy as she became a witness to Christ's resurrection and told others what she had seen. Peter's denial of Jesus before the cock crowed turned to joy as Jesus affirmed him on the beach and gave him the role of caring for his community. Thomas' faith deepened when he saw Jesus in person, which led to his commission to tell the gospel message to all those who would never touch Jesus themselves. The two disciples on their way to Emmaus, who felt a sense of hopelessness because of what had happened, discovered hope and life on their journey. Immediately, they set off to tell the disciples what had happened, which led to a renewed hope and joy amongst those disciples. What is your calling or mission?

"Even had there been no fall, God in his own limitless, outgoing love would still have chosen to identify himself with his creation by becoming man".[75] Although we cannot know for sure what would have happened had we not sinned, I think it is possible that God always intended to become man and dwell with us, in tune with his loving nature. Contemplate this understanding of God, that his desire was always to dwell with us and enter humanity. We understand that God has always desired to dwell with humanity and be in communion with us. He has always desired for humanity to join with him in taking stewardship of the world. As we consider our formation, it can be good not just to focus on the wonder of being forgiven and saved, but on the daily sanctifying work of the Spirit who forms us because of love and desire for relationship. Also to realise we each have a purpose, given by God, to work according to his will. For each of us, it will be different, depending on our gifts and abilities, but as Jesus lived in service to his Father, so we seek our vocation and work to serve God, rather than ourselves. This is key in the formation process, as we seek to understand our identity in Christ and worship God through all we are and made to be.

Reflection

Reflect on Christ's overflowing life, given to you like a fountain. His body and blood in the bread and the wine feed life to your body, soul, and spirit. Reflect not only on his crucifixion, and body given for you, but receive his life that feeds and sustains. Christ did not have to come to earth to save and sanctify us, but he chose to out of love. He showed us how to be human, and when we eat his body and blood we too choose to be sanctified and made more fully human. Thank Holy Spirit that he dwells with you, loves you unconditionally, and helps you in every way, and his desire is to draw you deeper in love with Jesus.

Scripture

The scripture for *Imaginative Prayer* today is John 21, which is set on the beach. The disciples are fishing when they see Jesus from a distance. They immediately drop everything they are doing and race back to the shore where Jesus is cooking breakfast for them. Their desire for Jesus overwhelms any interest in fishing. They spend time together with Jesus and he confirms the calling which is on their lives. Do we do what we hear Jesus asking us to do, so that all we do is fruitful to him? In *Imaginative Prayer* you read the scripture several times, until you have the story in your mind, then put the scripture aside and reflect on the story in your mind. Play the story back as you reflect and imagine what is going on. Are you in the boat with the disciples, or are you one of the disciples? Do you race to the shore, or are you already on the shore cooking fish and bread with Jesus? Does Jesus offer you fish and bread? Does he speak to you? How does the scene unfold? What do you feel?

Before you start reading, consider how God is looking at you with great love. Pray for God's grace as you enter the passage and pray that the risen Lord's own joy and gladness might come upon you and surprise you. Read the passage several times, letting the scene sink into your mind until you can set the Bible aside and enter the scene with your imagination.

At the end of your prayer time talk with Jesus, as with a dearly loved friend. Thank him for who he is and what he has done for you, and how he has led you in *Imaginative Prayer*. Journal the outcome.

Poem
Today, reflect on "The Peace Prayer of Saint Francis of Assisi".

Examen
Reflect on when you felt moved towards God and his love, and when you felt distant from him, which resulted in you feeling sad or uncomfortable. What are you most grateful for and what are you least grateful for this day? What brought you life and closer to God, and what drained you of life and led you away from God? Offer these moments to God in prayer and thankfulness that you can talk to him, and he listens. If you have children, you may like to do the *Examen* together, or you may like to do the *Examen* with another individual. Journal the outcome.

Day 30

Re-Creation

Contemplation

Every human being who comes into the world is made in the image of God but born "in Adam".[76] This phrase "in Adam" means that we all have a sinful nature, and we are all going to die. We have no choice in this matter. Due to Adam and Eve's rebellion, and because all humanity comes from their family, this is our inheritance. However, through Christ's life, death, resurrection, and ascension, we have been re-united into a loving relationship with the Father, through Jesus Christ.

After Jesus ascended into heaven to be with his Father, he sent Holy Spirit to live with those who receive him. Holy Spirit is the third person of the God Trinity. He saves and sanctifies us, uniting us with God the Father, through Christ the Son. When we receive Holy Spirit into our lives, we become participants in Christ's life and reign. We are no longer under the rule of sin and death "in Adam", but we live in Christ by the Holy Spirit.

When we understand we are no longer living "in Adam", in sin and death, but we are living in the loving embrace of life in Christ, our identity and purpose in life changes. We learn and understand that Jesus has shown us a new way to be human, and Holy Spirit is a gift to each person who believes in Jesus. He is the Son of God, and the result of his crucifixion, resurrection, and ascension, is eternal life for every Christian in the Trinity's loving embrace. Do you understand your true identity in Christ, and how loved you are? You have a purpose in life, and with Christ you can work and live to God's glory.

Jesus said, "I am the way, and the truth, and the life."[77] Interwoven throughout the biblical story is the story of Jesus Christ, the Son of God, who saves the world from sin and death. If we do not understand the biblical story, we limit ourselves in understanding the relationship of Father, Son, and Holy Spirit, and the immense love that God has for us, who has loved humanity from the beginning. If we do not understand the biblical story, then we cannot begin to understand how the Father has been lovingly fulfilling his purposes through the human race since creation started, and how this still continues. God's character and the vocation of humanity have not changed, as he desires for us still to be holy priests, stewarding his creation, and bringing justice to the world as we share this responsibility with Jesus by the Holy Spirit. If we are not aware of the biblical story, it is difficult to grasp who Father, Son, and Holy Spirit are, and why we were made. We misunderstand what God has been doing throughout history, and how his purpose has always been for us to partner with him in love and purpose. If we do not live in the biblical story, we are living in our own story, for ourselves or for others, and the culture of the fallen world around us.

There will be a day when Jesus Christ will come again to earth. When he comes, he will deal completely with sin, death, Satan, and evil for all time. He will fully restore and renew humanity and all creation. He will redeem all that is decaying and dying, so all creation will be redeemed and fully restored to a new creation. We will live in a relationship with God and be the true image-bearers we were always meant to be. We will live in perfect peace and harmony with one another as we care for creation and partner with King Jesus in his purposes over the world. Our bodies will be transformed to be like Christ's resurrection body; we will have a physical body able to eat and drink and which is renewed to live forever with Christ. Creation will give birth to its true potential, which God always desired, and we will rule as wise stewards over all of creation with Jesus as our King. This dying, decaying world will not be destroyed, as some think, but transformed, and we, the church, are a part of this future reality, even as we live in the present. We eternally partner with God in caring for creation and the purposes he has for us.

God's purpose for creation is not just for the future. As agents and signposts to God's grace and love, we contribute to transforming God's world now, in the power of the Holy Spirit. Through whatever vocation we have, we can pray and act in the power of the Holy Spirit to bring redemption and restoration to this earth. We are God's temple on earth, declaring his gospel message to the world. This includes being with the poor and wounded to help restore them, as well as looking after God's beautiful creation, and not contributing to the destruction of that which God made good. As Christ's body, the church and potential stewards of God's creation in the new creation, we can enter that vocation now; we are to build the kingdom of God and model justice and peace. As Paul says in 1 Corinthians 15, what we do now is not in vain because "each one's work will become manifest, for the Day will disclose it".[78] There is a continuity between what we do in this present life, and what God will give to us in the future.

Reflection

How is Holy Spirit transforming you? Do you see yourself as a wise steward partnering with Holy Spirit over creation? What is your vocation? Talk to Jesus about this as you would with a dearly loved friend. You may want to end with the following response of gratitude before you journal the outcome.

> Take, Lord, and receive all my liberty, my memory, my understanding, and my entire will, all that I have and possess. You gave it all to me; to you I return it. All is yours, dispose of it entirely according to your will. Give me only the love of you together with your grace, for that is enough for me.[79]

Scripture

The scripture for *Imaginative Prayer* today is the ascension of Christ in Acts 1:1-11. In *Imaginative Prayer* you read the scripture several times until you have the story in your mind, then put the scripture aside and reflect on the story in your mind. Before you start reading, consider how God is looking at you with great love. Pray for God's grace as you enter the passage and pray that the risen Lord's own joy and gladness might come upon you and surprise you. Read the passage several times, letting the scene sink into your mind until you can set the Bible aside and enter the scene with your imagination. Reflect on what is happening as you imagine yourself there. What do you experience? What do you do? What do you hear? What do you feel? What do you say? Does Jesus speak to you?

At the end of your prayer time talk with Jesus, as with a dearly loved friend. Thank him for who he is and what he has done for you, and how he has led you in *Imaginative Prayer*. Journal the outcome.

Poem
The final poem for these thirty days of contemplation is another reflection on creation by Mary Oliver, called "The Ponds".

Examen
Reflect on when you felt moved towards God and his love, and when you felt distant from him, which resulted in you feeling sad or uncomfortable. For what are you most grateful and for what are you least grateful this day? What brought you life and closer to God, and what drained you of life and led you away from God? Offer these moments to God in prayer and thankfulness that you can talk to him, and he listens. If you have children, you may like to do the *Examen* together, or you may like to do the *Examen* with another individual. Journal the outcome.

End Notes

---

[1] Luke 5:16.

[2] Mark 6:31.

[3] Foster, R. J., & Smith, J. B. (Eds.). (2005), *Devotional Classics: Selected Readings for Individuals and Groups* (Rev. and expanded), HarperSanFrancisco, p. 81.

[4] Galatians 2:20.

[5] Romans 8:6.

[6] Hebrews 4:12.

[7] Luke 24:30-31.

[8] Romans 12:2.

[9] Genesis 1:27.

[10] Carver, J. (2015), *Ignatian Spirituality and Ecology: Entering into Conversation with the Earth. 4*, 10, p. 7.

[11] John 8:12.

[12] 1 John 4:8.

[13] Webber, R. E. (2006), *The Divine Embrace: Recovering the Passionate Spiritual Life*, Baker Books, p. 25.

[14] Keating, T. (2006), *The Method of Centering Prayer*, Contemplative Outreach, Ltd. https://www.contemplativeoutreach.org/centering-prayer-method/

[15] Genesis 1:1.

[16] John 1:1.

[17] Genesis 1:31.

[18] John 6:39-40.

[19] Webber, R. E. (2006), *The Divine Embrace: Recovering the Passionate Spiritual Life*, Baker Books. p. 16.

[20] Psalm 27:4.

[21] Webber, R. E. (2006), *The Divine Embrace: Recovering the Passionate Spiritual Life*, Baker Books, p. 103.

[22] Jones, B. D. (2014), *Dwell: Life with God for the World*, IVP, p. 119.

[23] Ibid., p. 145.

[24] Ibid., p. 143.

[25] Ephesians 1:4.

[26] Hughes, G. W. (1994), *God of Surprises* (28th printing), Darton Longman and Todd, p. 55-63.

[27] Ignatius, & Ivens, M. (2004), *The Spiritual Exercises of Saint Ignatius of Loyola*, Gracewing; Inigo Enterprises, p. 11.

[28] Augustine, (1996), *The Confessions of St. Augustine*, Whitaker House, p.11.

[29] Romans 8:39.

[30] Matthew 6:10.

[31] Genesis 2:3.

[32] Jones, B. D. (2014), *Dwell: Life with God for the World*, IVP, p. 161.

[33] Ibid., p. 53.

[34] Ibid., p. 63.

[35] Psalm 139.

[36] Jones, B. D. (2014), *Dwell: Life with God for the World*, IVP, p. 70.

[37] John 6:63.

[38] Romans 8:29.

[39] 2 Corinthians 2:18.

[40] Philippians 2:7-8.

[41] Mark 5:26.

[42] Augustinus, A., Lawler, T. C., & Augustinus, A. (1978), *Sermons for Christmas and Epiphany* (Nachdr.d. Ausg. New York: Paulist, 1952), Newman, p. 107, Sermon 191.

[43] Ware, M. K. (2018), *The Orthodox Way*, St Vladimir's Seminary Press, p. 100.

[44] Ibid., p. 108.

[45] Luke 2:26.

[46] Ibid., 2:21.

[47] Ibid., 2:39.

[48] Ibid., 2:52.

[49] Ibid., 2:40.

[50] Matthew 3:13-17.

[51] John 5:19.

[52] Matthew 3:17.

[53] Goggin, J., & Strobel, K. (2017), *The Way of the Dragon or the Way of the Lamb: Searching for Jesus' Path of Power in a Church that has Abandoned it*, Thomas Nelson, p. 13.

[54] Galatians 5:1.

[55] Palmer, P. J. (2000), *Let Your Life Speak: Listening for the Voice of Vocation*, Jossey-Bass, p. 10.

[56] Ibid., p. 15.

[57] Ibid., p. 48-49.

[58] *Wedding vows*, (2023, February 27), The Church of England. https://www.churchofengland.org/life-events/your-church-wedding/planning-your-ceremony/wedding-vows

[59] Smith, J. K. A. (2016), *You are What you Love: The Spiritual Power of Habit*, Brazos Press, p. 2.

[60] Augustine, (1996), *The Confessions of St. Augustine,* Whitaker House, p. 11.

[61] John 15

[62] Acts 20:35

[63] Ignatius, & Ivens, M. (2004), *The Spiritual Exercises of Saint Ignatius of Loyola*, Gracewing; Inigo Enterprises, p. 69.

[64] Keating, T. (2006), *The Method of Centering Prayer*, Contemplative Outreach, Ltd., https://www.contemplativeoutreach.org/centering-prayer-method/

[65] Ignatius, & Ivens, M. (2004), *The Spiritual Exercises of Saint Ignatius of Loyola*, Gracewing; Inigo Enterprises, p. 69.

[66] Ibid., p. 69.

[67] Genesis chapters 2-3.

[68] Hebrew 1:3.

[69] Webber, R. E. (2006), *The Divine Embrace: Recovering the Passionate Spiritual Life*, Baker Books, p. 135.

[70] Ignatius, & Ivens, M. (2004), *The Spiritual Exercises of Saint Ignatius of Loyola*, Gracewing; Inigo Enterprises, p. 69.

[71] Rolheiser, R. (2010, March 28), *The Humiliation of Crucifixion | Ron Rolheiser.* https://ronrolheiser.com/the-humiliation-of-crucifixion/

[72] Wansbrough, H. (Ed.). (1999), *The New Jerusalem Bible* (Pocket ed., [reprint.]), Darton, Longman & Todd.

[73] Julian of Norwich, (1966). *Julian of Norwich: Revelations of Divine Love* (C. Wolters, Trans.), Penguin Books, p. 68.

[74] Webber, R. E. (2006), *The Divine Embrace: Recovering the Passionate Spiritual Life*, Baker Books, p. 135.

75 Ware, M. K. (2018), *The Orthodox Way*, St Vladimir's Seminary Press, p. 100.

76 1 Corinthians 15:21-22.

77 John 14:6.

78 I Corinthians 3:13.

79 Ignatius, & Ivens, M. (2004), *The Spiritual Exercises of Saint Ignatius of Loyola*, Gracewing; Inigo Enterprises, p. 69.

Printed in Great Britain
by Amazon

41653957R00078